Gazin' West

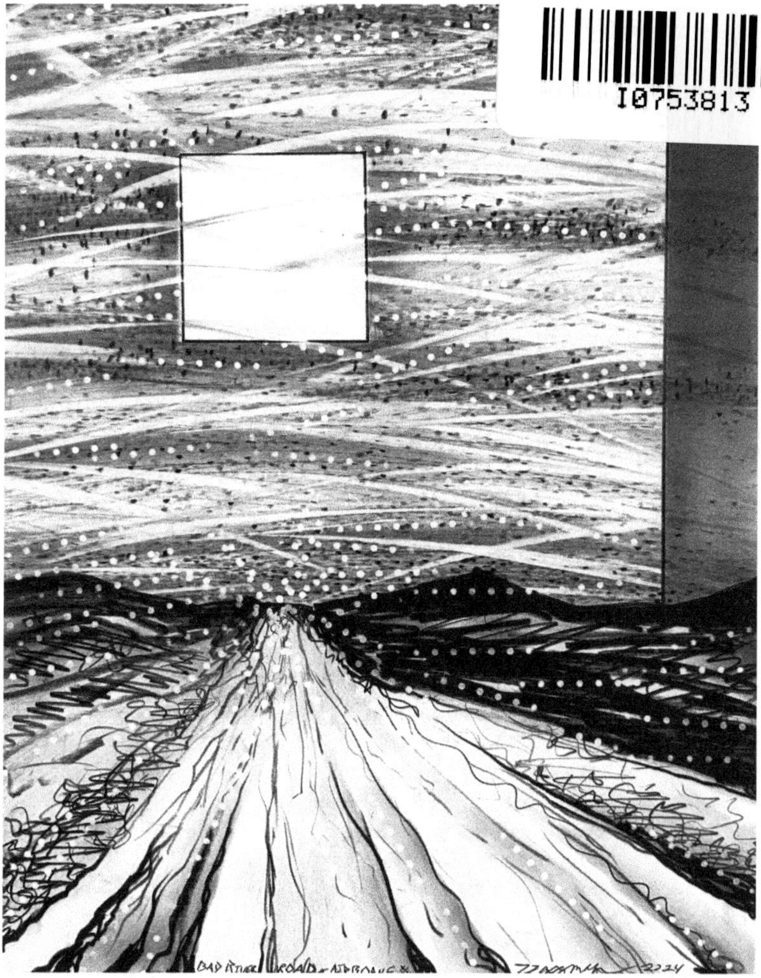

poems by Lin Marshall Brummels

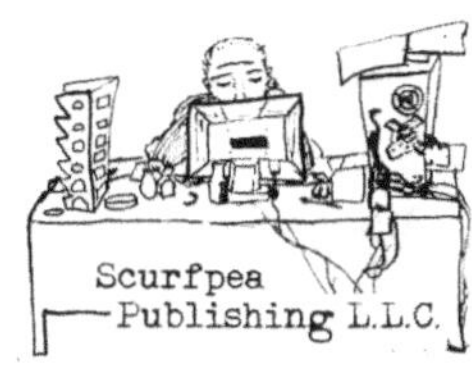

Cover artwork: Mark Zimmerman. *Bad River Road – Sky Box.*
25.5" x 19.5", watercolor and gouache on Murillo.

Dusty billowing gold climbs,
finds a broken gap,
and vanishes beneath a distant cloud
that floats endlessly away.
Bury the day. It's done for.
Night crouches in a box,
spills out each shadowy evening,
creeping into waiting silence,
marching away to coyote calls,
laughing all the way. – Mark Zimmerman

First Edition 2026

Scurfpea Publishing LLC
P.O. Box 46
Sioux Falls, SD 57101
scurfpeapublishing.com
editor@scurfpeapublishing.com

Poems

Artwork

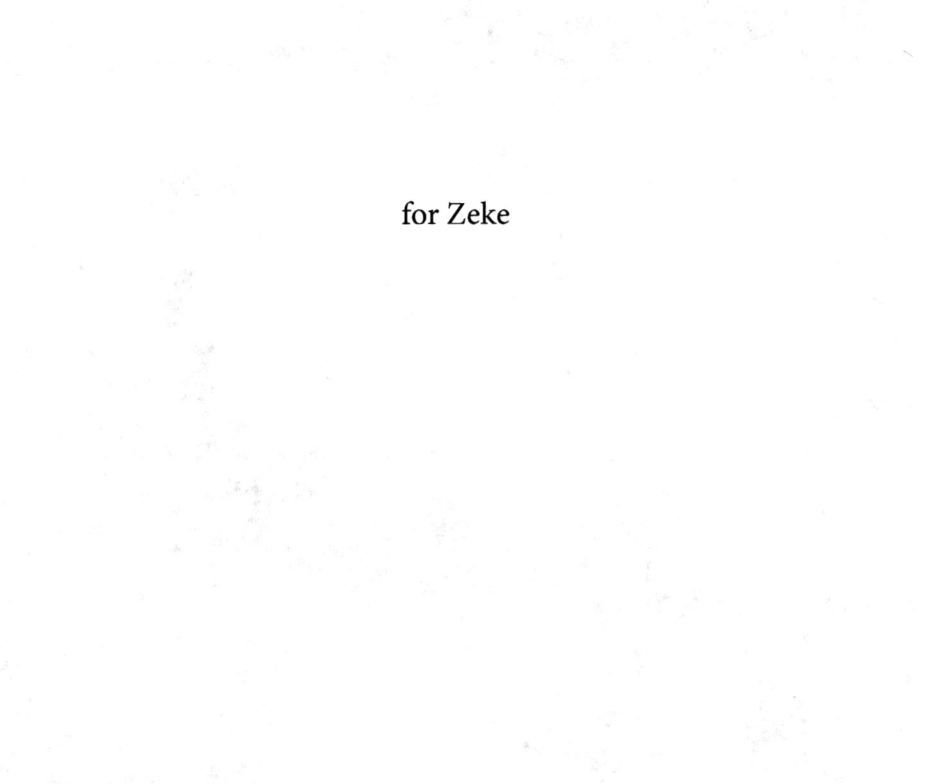

for Zeke

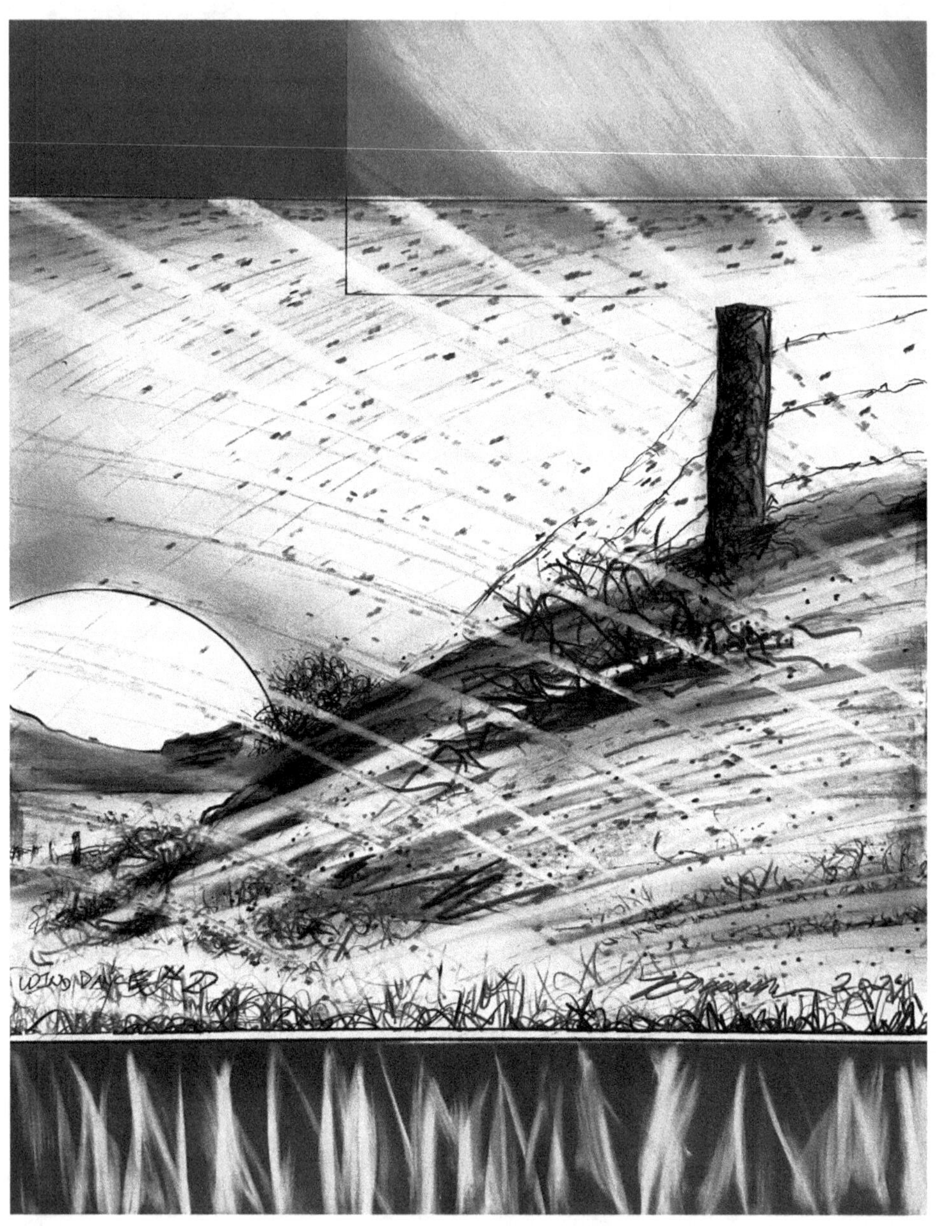

First Love

I knew his first love was a horse,
trained when they were both colts.
That old horse carried me on rides by his side,
ferried his younger brothers through their teen years
and lived to be thirty or more.

It was clear that he loved horses more than me,
brought another into our life before we had kids,
trained the new mare to ride,
grinned wide when she birthed a big strapping son
as our baby boy arrived.

He taught our son and the new colt
to be one with nature,
live as if there were no tomorrow,
welcomed me to join them with a horse of my own,
a gentle old roan named Blue.

Gazin' West

after Lyn Denaeyer's *Breaking Even*

He might set on the steps of an evenin'
trying to settle in his mind a way
to make peace with this compromise,
a way to do something with this piece
of clay in the middle of corn country.
It is not the vision he held on to those
years in eastern colleges, not the view
he had in mind when he thought of cows
grazing, not his idea of where to ride.
He might have a beer or two out there,
gazin' off to the west where his heart
planned to rest, riding in short grass
pastures too big to see perimeter fence.
Settling here was a way to make it work
with her, a way to raise a family, drive
to a city job, all those trappings of life
he wanted, too, but it hurt just the same
to understand he couldn't always do it
his way. He might sit out there a bit
some days till the call of the west
calmed, while he worked on a plan
to turn these cornfields into grassland.

Tank

Our fourth-grade grins
carried us horseback,
cantering sandy streets
of our hometown, flirting
as only ten-year-old's can.
You went to work on nuclear
reactors in Germany
for the Army, earned your
nickname, Tank, bulldozing
your way from one assignment
to another. I followed
my passion to research dung
beetles. You called when
you were in town, we
met for dinner for a while.
Bib-wearing farmer you became,
gave you a perfect opportunity
to get elected to Commissioner,
oversee roads for three counties.
I followed my beetles from toilets
to swamps, had a brief flirtation
with oceanography.
Alone later in life I wondered
why you stopped calling until
a friend sent your obituary;
it said your ashes were scattered.
Without a marked grave
your memory floats free
like the ghosts of horses
we used to ride.

Rhyming on Horseback

The blind appaloosa, the quarter horse no one rides
and the high-stepping-leader-of-the-pack mare
nicker when they smell sweet ripe apples waiting
in the feed bunk, lower their heads and crunch
in unison. I'm captivated by their musical dipping
and chewing, imagine writing poems on horseback,
some that rhyme and others that don't, reading
in public like I can do now, but was too shy to do
when horses and I were young.

In those early days, I wish I tried out the idea
of writing on horseback, but children, jobs
and, frankly, the whimsical idea itself kept
my feet on the ground. Now, my hips and knee
tell me that hefting a saddle atop a tall horse
is best left to those with strong upper arms,
cinch tightening to those with enough muscle
to pull the leather taut so saddle doesn't slip,
and it's tough to balance a laptop up there anyway.

Pocket Song

Good morning starshine
The earth says hello
You twinkle above us
We twinkle below – Oliver

My garden shirt has oversized
pockets front and back
to haul tomatoes and peppers
from the veggie patch.

I stitch the back ones
to give the shirt stability
and conjure a pop song.
Its melody sticks in my head.

I carry the lyrics in my pockets.
It's my song of praise
for all things Mother Nature
provides in my lucky life.

There's food in the fridge,
a roof over my head, two
grown kids off on a journey
of their own, a dog in her bed,

horses graze in the meadow,
hooves clip, clop as they walk.
Gliddy, glop, gloopy, I feel
happy to meet the morning.

Chins, Withers, and Whiskers

Mom hated her chin whiskers,
asked me to tweeze them
when she was bed-ridden.

Yellow cat likes chin scratches,
stands on my lap to remind me
he's been neglected.

Horses prefer withers' strokes.
Comb horses' manes beginning
at their withers, remove mud,

burs, and tangles. Give
West Nile shots high
on those withers, opposite

equine mane's natural part.
Calico cat is losing her whiskers,
and ability to sense openings,

wants the door held wide
to come and go safely, doesn't
care for chin scratches.

Now I, too, have chin whiskers
plucked by my hairdresser.
Mom never had that choice.

Moving the Herd

after Margot Liberty's *Evening, Four Mile*

Incredible, the softness of the air
this Labor Day morn as mammas
call to their calves, all early risers.

The herd settles the day after moving.
There was a time when pastures
were nearby, open grassland

plentiful and family on horseback
moved cattle from one paddock
to the next; now grassland is plowed,

fields planted to three-dollar corn,
farmers gambling their crops will yield,
others will fail, corn prices improve.

Herd arrives, seventeen calves
in a trailer and the rest in a semi pot
all trailing their personal fly vortex.

No stranger to flies, one buzzes my head.
I flail at it ineffectually, separated
from myself yet welcome the herd.

Cool morning air calms. Mommas
find their babies for breakfast, ignore
flies we will all fight till hard frost.

Coyote Chaser's Daughter

Coyote stops
looks directly at me
Her eyes hold me accountable – Linda Hussa, *Under the Hunter Moon*

Coyote Chaser flanked the night herd,
moved sleepy babies back to cuddle with their mothers.

That old mamma cow did not allow
measly coyotes to molest her or any of herd's calves.

A Long Horn, Angus cross, she was tough.
None lived longer than Coyote Chaser who stole the breeze.

Now her daughter has the job of stirring the wind,
making tornados in my coffee cup. Clinging to my perch,

I hold tight to watch from barn roof
lest the windstorm topples me over the edge.

Coyote Chaser's Daughter dips her horns,
rangy coyotes back off, knowing when they are beaten.

Once in a Blue Nebraska Moon

The 2009 Blue Moon was far rarer than usual,
because it happened right on New Year's Eve –
a coincidence that happens only once in every twenty years. – Rosa Golijan

Below zero at dusk
when I check the horse's water,
watch the blue New Year's Eve moon
rise over frozen white fields,
snow drifts shift in winter wind,
tree, animal, human shadows
visible in the moon's blush.

Horses circle the trough,
restless after days confined
behind drifts that blocked
their pathway to pasture.
They break through the snow,
stretch their legs on the way
to water, oats, hay.

Cows huddle by the barn,
desperate for space,
but wait for humans
to provide drink, feed,
salvation from winter's face.

Cracks in the tank's ice cover
from repeated attempts
to break through,
mirror shadowy outlines
cast by the moon's glow.

Trees, animals look like spectral
versions of themselves; my breath
frozen in the still air a ghostly gasp:
am I waiting to be saved like cows
    or a horse
    taking this rare chance to explore?

Prairie Post

After *Reply Requested* by Herb Mignery

She patiently waited some days, other times she paced
back and forth with the baby in her arms,
eyes continually darting to the window,
peering out to search the horizon for a possible visitor,
a neighbor passing on the trip to town
or better on the way home as there may have been
a package or letter sent her way.

She wrote to several relatives in Philadelphia
last month, to her mother in Syracuse
a week after that and to an old friend
recently moved to Chicago with her new husband,
closing each missive with *reply requested.*
She wrote a letter to the editor of the Denver Post
about the shocking costs of sugar and flour.

She inwardly fumed that her correspondents
didn't appreciate how anxiously she awaited each response,
perhaps not realizing how far she lived from any town,
how seldom she was able to leave home, three children
under five requiring all her time,
husband gone days and many nights cowboying
for the big ranch down the road.

She reached out to absently pet the dog,
thought about the last time she read a newspaper,
tried to recall the last time all three children were asleep,
chores done and it was light enough to read
the Bible or one of the books she kept hidden
from the little boys' boisterous play, her daughter's tiny fingers.

She found time to write a quick note to her sister
in Omaha about the petite red flowers just now blooming
near the barn. She wrote about the baby's first step,
her oldest son's attempt to climb the hay loft ladder, his fall,
how thankful she was that he did not break any bones,
ended the missive *reply requested*, sent the message
with her neighbor, kind enough to stop for mail on his trip to town.

Saturday Ride

It's no trick to get killed ranching.
You might get a foot caught
in a stirrup when your horse bucks,
get dragged to death . . . – Linda Hasselstrom, *Rancher Roulette*

"Get me a beer
when you're in the fridge,
I don't want a miss this play,"
he demands.

"Damn it's cold outside.
The mare busted a rein.
I nearly lost my stirrup when she
loped under that cottonwood north of the gate,

and then a damn deer
ran out of the trees to the west
right across our path and Hoss's
mount shied away from the herd.

It's the fricking wind today,
all of them a little spooky,
lucky nobody got hurt,
all got back in one piece."

She listens patiently,
nods affirmation, grabs beers,
offers one to all,
returns to read her fantasy.

A handsome Scottish highlander
time travels to sweep
her off her feet,
tell her she's beautiful.

Horse Thief

They moved to a hard-scrabble Keya Paha county ranch
with five kids, she raised them alone in a two room
tarpaper tenant shack, prairie wind howling through the walls
after he froze to death cowboying in the blizzard of '88.

Kids left Sandhills country at an early age,
made their way in life; oldest daughter married young,
moved away, two sons next in line hired out to wrangle cows,
a fourth died of a fever and the last, named Bert, saw the lay
of the land, headed out to find another way to get by.

Bert was a natural born rider, a wunderkind who tamed
any mount for pay, but quit working, took up horse thieving
as more profitable and fun, courted a reputation
thereabouts for borrowing animals.

Caught and convicted as a horse thief at nineteen,
served time in the Nebraska State Pen beginning in '01,
checked in to serve the sentence at five feet eight inches tall,
140 pounds, Bert claimed to be a married man,
worked in the prison broom factory, performed
duties well according to prison records.

It's uncertain how Bert's condition was hidden, unclear
how the guards failed to notice through admittance bath,
physical exam, living with hardened men for eleven long months
that Bert was really a young lady named Lena.

The prison doctor confirmed the story that Bert nee Lena was a she,
her gender revealed after she spurned her cellmate's advances.
Amused at the fuss, Lena requested a dress to replace her suit of stripes
for the move to the women's reformatory.

Governor Savage heard the story, pardoned Lena
on condition she reform her ways,
return to Springview, live with her mother
for the rest of her days.

Found

sorting cows, canners, and keepers
you hate final decisions – Thelma Poirer, *sorting cattle*

From calving to weaning
there are decisions,
will the momma cow allow you close
enough to ear-tag, check for gender.
Before calves are too large,
separate from their mommas for branding,
cutting. Listen to cows
call for their babies,
drown out voices
of cowhands calling for shots,
sharp knife to cut the bulls,
branding iron to add your mark.
The count is off – a pair is missing.
Two cowhands fork saddle horses,
search the green hills
flush with spring brome,
find the baby, still-born,
grieving momma standing guard.

Horses Paint a Pretty Picture

What he loved in horses was what he loved in men,
the blood and the heat of the blood that ran them. – Cormac McCarthy,
All the Pretty Horses

Horses have been painted on cave walls since people found a way to record their stories and, now, they occupy our collective imagination. Poems, novels, and songs keep equine legends alive. Wealthy families have always had their own carriage horses to pull buggies and sleighs around cities and to travel to their country homes. Teams pulled stagecoaches filled with passengers as the population moved west from eastern cities. Breeders developed specialty horses for racing, like Thoroughbreds and Tennessee Walkers. Quarter Horses are associated with cowboys and barbwire wars for control of the American West. The west coast Nez Perce tribe domesticated a spotted breed they called Appaloosas. Spanish explorers left horses behind to fend for themselves when they didn't find gold in the American southwest. Those feral western plains equines with Spanish heritage interbred with lost eastern thoroughbreds and evolved into tall, swift ponies. Stallions gathered bands of mares, ran wild. Western tribes tamed those mounts, painted their horses and their faces to mark their brand. Wild steeds lent them legs to extend their geography, giving native warriors a fighting chance.

Huge draft horses, like Percherons and Clydesdales, have gone to war with us many times to tug cannons into battle, to carry away our wounded, and our dead. Gifted trainers show these gentle giants at state fair competitions today to demonstrate team horsemanship. Horses carried Pony Express Riders swiftly between stops to deliver the mail for the short time it was in operation. Ranchers rode and still ride horses to herd cattle across vast pastures. Farmers hitched nags to plows to break native sod, kids rode ponies to school to learn easier ways to live, and now saddlehorses carry us on pleasure rides. Today, teams of riders give calf-roping demonstrations at rodeos. My aging hay burners paint a pretty picture doing nothing but munching on prairie hay, ambling to the re-planted native grass pasture, and napping in sunshine.

Pay attention to history
Avoid get-rich schemes
Sit in sunshine, enjoy the day

Laced With Whiskey

Their house has a story
that would not have occurred
had they stayed. It would not
have become a brothel for a season
and we would not
have befriended a spotted dog
abandoned by a john.

Another friend would not have lived there,
tamed a wild horse in his corral.
We would not have drunk his coffee
laced with whiskey
on our twentieth anniversary,
earned the mother of all hangovers.

He would not have gotten the job
vacated by their move.
Our kids would not have received
benefit of his mentoring.
House would not now be used
to birth baby goats, store old clothes,
chicken feeders, heat lamps.

Another Fall

The dead rise like bubbles – Roberta Gould, *Reverse*

Neil adopted a sickly appaloosa
thirty-odd years ago, named
her Ghost, she was so thin
he didn't think she had a ghost
of a chance to live.

Ghost has been boarding here
since her knee went bad.
She can't carry him herding
cows, trail riding, or hunting.

She's been susceptible to falling,
slipping on ice, becoming
stuck in mucky manure, and
lately stumbling over dry grass.

When she falls on her bad leg,
she needs help to flip over
on her good leg, allowing her
to get up on her own.

Another fall today begs
the question of when she finally goes,
will her ghost come alive,
rise like the bubbles foaming
around her mouth when prone?

Sentinel

Rented hill pasture plowed,
planted to corn this season.

Husband saved a Ponderosa
volunteering in the grass.

He paid a tree mover
to bring it home, planted it

on a hilltop overlooking the barns,
watered it with tender loving care.

Then he left and, like the grassland,
he has gone, not to return.

The pine remains as seasons pass,
sitting on the hill's crest,

overlooking snowy-terraced
remnants of summer grass.

It marks his favorite mare's grave,
weathered halter hangs nearby.

Paying homage to their sister,
horses graze ice-covered stems,

munch on standing alfalfa,
big bluestem, little blue,

and Indian grass seed heads
missed last summer.

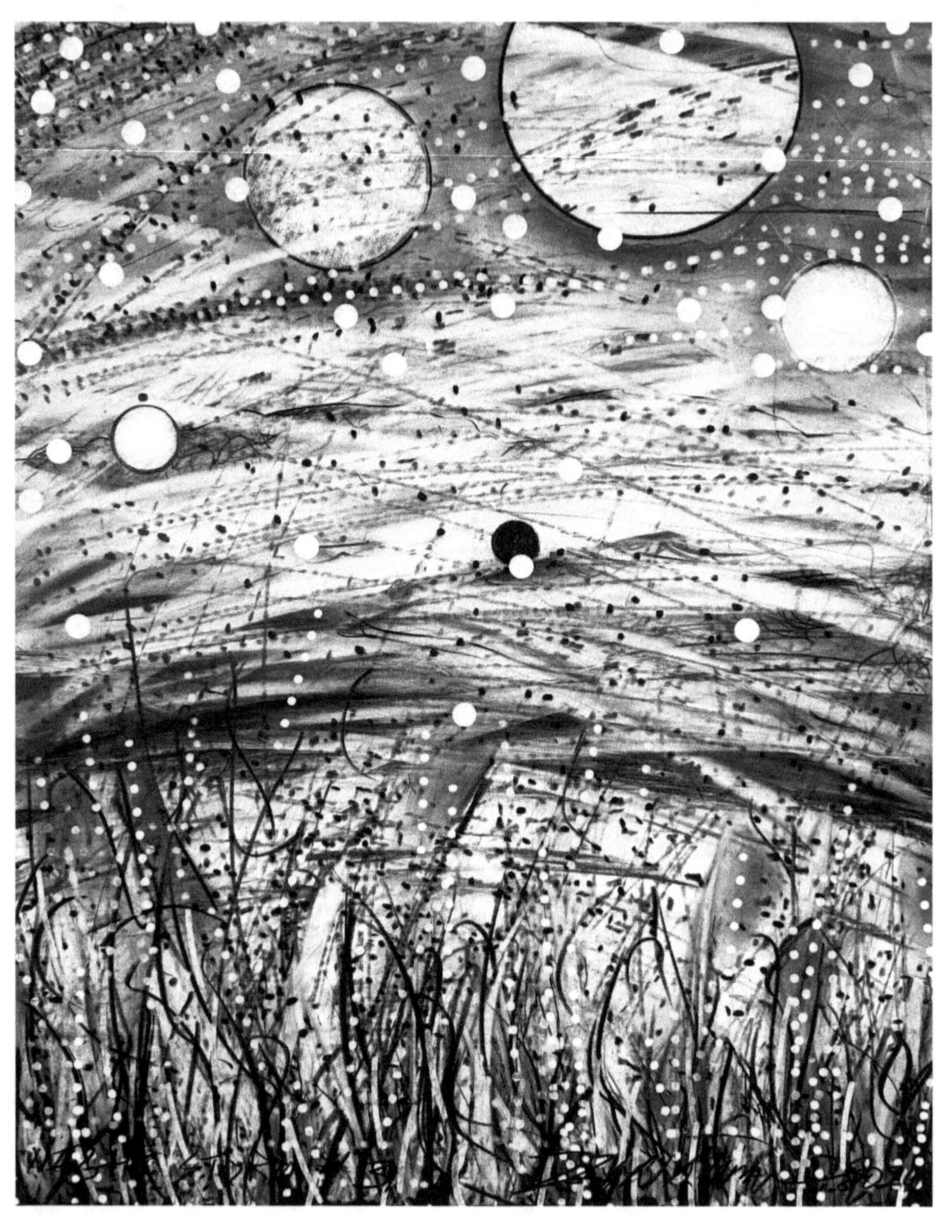

Solstice Celebration

Let's give thanks to the Lord
because Santa Claus comes tonight – Bob Dylan, *Here Comes Santa Claus*

Kittens scamper from countertop
to table and back,
circle through house plants,
Christmas tree branches.
They scatter leaves, ornaments,
entertain me
before I go outside,
feed horses' extra oats, apples.
Lowering my head to fight
howling north winds,
hustling through daily chores,
I smile at sight of the woodpile,
fueling the stove,
radiating heat to thaw
fingers beginning to numb,
warm my chilly cheeks.
Dylan's songs entertain,
windows steam,
temps plummet,
gifts wrapped,
parties attended,
goodies delivered.
All checked off the to-do list.
Time to enjoy a pot of tea,
call a friend, pet the cats,
and pack for a tropical vacation.

Wild Herds

Winter wind lovingly
greets old man January
as he trudges down slopes
from the highland, dragging
a bag of lost fallen stars.
His magic powder sprinkles
moldy covers of old horse books.
Mare's graze peacefully nearby.
Seeking answers, determined early
pilgrims also search
for the missing gold key
that turns the lock rusty from disuse.

Travelers pursuing wisdom hear tales
of hidden silver rivers
flowing over ancient boulders.
They believe stories fulfill
prophets' predictions
of secret meadows
filled with wild herds.

Apache's War

Zeke named his horse Apache,
his go-to mount for many years.
Equine poked his eyes on spiky brome
during a drought, trying to get
a few bites of green grass.
Dr. Melissa examined Apache,
diagnosed corneal ulcers
from injuries and likely to be
sensitive to light. Doc advocated
use of a fly mask and/or keeping him
in a darkened stall until healed.
We cleaned the barn, cleared
a stall away from sunlight,
doctored his eyes daily.
At first, Apache agreed to fight
his way back to sight. However,
he warred against the dark stall,
eye medicine, and the mask.
Finally, relenting, we turned him
out to pasture, he promptly ditched
the mask, never to be found.
Apache, mostly blind, navigated
grasslands running with other horses
for the rest of his days.

The word "Apache" comes from the Yuma word for "fighting-men"
and from the Zuni word meaning "enemy."

Horse Circus

Two more horses arrive
one frigid January day

to board with the others.
The Appaloosa, Apache,

protecting his home territory,
spars with the incoming gelding.

New mare, lame with arthritis,
hangs back out of the fray.

Apache bites, then crashes
into this interloper, forcing

him to the corner of the corral.
Snow flies, bodies collide

as they chase each other
around and about. Wood fences

crack in the five-degree
cold as they write a new

manual of barnyard order.
Wrapped in winter's blanket,

watching this circus, I forget
my cold feet and believe

they will soon be friends,
unlike humans who hold onto rage.

Filament Rider

In my nightmare, riderless
horse stumbles into our yard,
from next door's windfarm.
Mare is covered with silver
barbwire crisscrossing
saddle where a rider should be.
Intricate barbwire design
looks like a hatted rider
until seen up-close.
Wire is blood splattered,
mare gaunt from the filament
burden she carries.
We begin the daunting task
of cutting away tangled barbs,
careful not to cause more harm.
Once mess is removed from girth,
stirrups, and untangled from horn,
rest lifts away.
Unsaddled, hapless horse
gratefully rolls, allows us
to lead her to water, pasture.
We turn to the barbwire form,
looking for all the world,
like a filament rider.

I awake mid-call
to the county sheriff
reporting bloody barbs.

The Crossing

Seven horses huddle south of the barn
during yet another snow

hoping more hay will magically appear
this late February day.

Walking over drifts covering the fence,
they create a crossing into the grove,

remembering summer grass.

They stroll over this barrier daily,
or more often, in search of food.

I watch them cross with trepidation,
wondering if one, then another

will be caught in the wires as snow
begins to slip slide away into spring.

February Mud

When snow melts in cities,
it leaves behind only a bit
of dirty white edges
in gutters and alleys.

Concrete walks and streets
dry nicely. Cars get washed.
People move easily,
work clothes stay clean.

Rural roads with scarce gravel
and dirt byways heave and buckle
when frost begins to thaw.
Need four-wheel drive to make it.

Corrals' icy, manurey corners
block drainage creating
clay-hay gooey muck
thick enough to make pottery.

You are splattered head to boot
with mud when choring,
trying to avoid
slipping and falling.

Horses tiptoe to feeders
for oats on icy mornings,
roll in mud-melt after
alfalfa supper.

You think again about moving
to a city with clean streets
and easy living but decide
against it, toast the day.

Just a Little Rain

After Elizabeth Ebert's, *An Ordinary Morning*

"Twas just an ordinary mornin"
like many other early spring days,
except a mite warmer. We were
hoping the cold spell was finally
broken to melt our foot of snow,
two or more out west when clouds
moved in bringing a rainstorm.
He joked as he'd often done before,
yep, a little rain will melt snow,
be easier for the old cows to calve,
help the new babies thrive.
Moisture will be widespread,
the forecasters said. We pulled
on our boots, hooded chore coats,
ventured out in the downpour
to feed the horses a dose of oats.
It warmed and poured for days,
snow melted and ran off frozen
ground across three states.
Riverbanks overflowed, moving
ice chunks size of cars, picking
up fallen tree trunks along the way,
stranding cattle, flooding homes,
pastures, closing roads, ruining
bridge supports and even taking out
an earthen dam out west. All that
water moved downstream over-
flowing rivers, one after another –
Elkhorn, Niobrara, Missouri,
Mississippi on toward the Gulf,
flooding farmland, towns, and cities
along the way. From now on, every
warm spring rain begs the question,
What could go wrong?

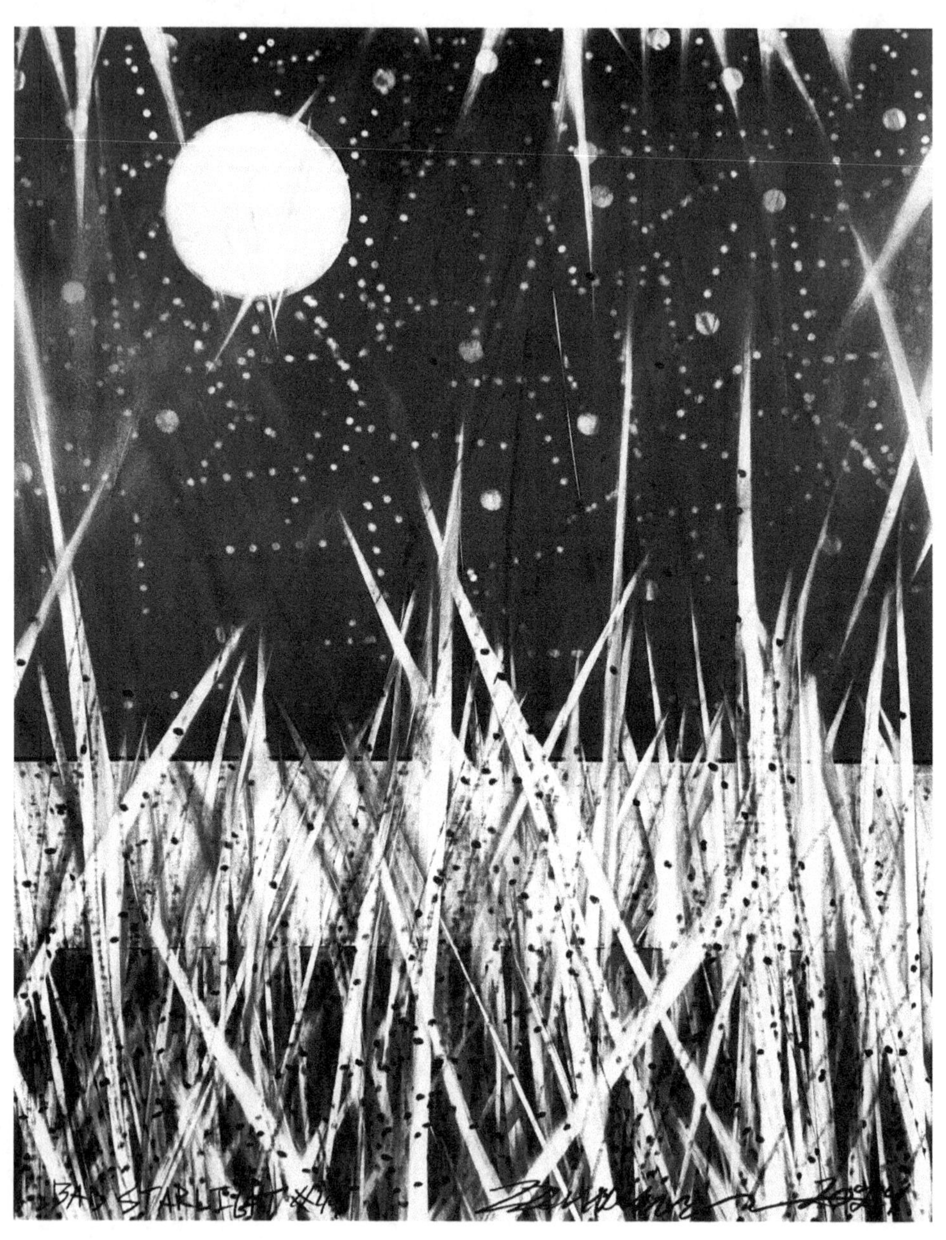
BAD STARLIGHT #4

Grass Moon

Young monarchs emerge.
April winds blow winged
beauties through well-timed
daffodils and budding birch.
Mare gallops, takes charge,
moves cattle in her own time.
Grass Moon shyly hides behind
overcast skies, storm surges.

I toss prairie grass seed over terrain,
finches cling to swinging feeders.
Each in our own way keen
to plant summer forage before rain.
Busy mare is a cheerleader,
urging cows toward new greens.

Planting

Storm cloud forms, early April tulips open.

Sheet lightning bolts flash, scare mares,
horses' neighs heard above drums' crash.

April fourteenth phone rings, *Taxes ready*.
Horse after horse wants grain. She drives
across storm's track, signs form, writes check.

With Arbor Day looming, tulips already blooming,
storm system receding, horses out to pasture,
she grasps the garden spade with tired back,
aging hands' prominent blue veins like her mother's.

Her body's discarded its eggs years ago,
now in spring sunshine, she plunges the blade deep
into yellow clay, lifts soil, sets it aside, repeats,
like she's searching for the earth's fertility
and discarding spent friable topsoil.

Finally, she excavates enough dirt to house
the waiting seedling, pulls the container
toward her, lifts out the dry-root stick, gently
settles it in the hole, adds water, compost, pats
soil in place, waters again, her blue veins
covered with muddy clay, and plants new life.

Fertile Ground

Horned Herford bull prefers
to rest on soft green grass pillows.
Black Angus is indifferent to place,
plops down where he pleases.
They are gardeners preparing to plant,
biding time to plow fallow ground,
just waiting for spring's fertility
to deposit those precious seeds.

Little bothered by rain or mud,
planting will be strategic, pointed.
Bulls will be in and out quickly.
They are bovine Johnny Appleseeds
fulfilling their destiny to seed orchards,
bring forth fruit to the land.

Calf Count

Sometimes we cross the river
on bad ice to check for calves because
one cow backed up to a wash and
dropped her calf into the water. – Gretel Ehrlich, *For David*

It was a tough winter, to hear the stories.
She was snowed-in for two weeks in January.
Son and his dad brought milk and bread,
horse feed by sled downhill from an open corner.
They fed cows round bales by tractor.
Horses at her place left to struggle
to reach oats she fought drifts to feed.
Spring arrived early by some accounts.
One calf found dead, one disappeared
from remote pastures checked when they could.
Finally counting calves in summer,
another has gone missing.
Rethinking the math, it is just an extra cow
to feed through another summer,
we pray she carries a calf to term this time.

Hideaways

As we rode down the hill, I got the creepy feeling you get
when you know somebody you can't see is watching you. – Trixie Belden,
Secret of the Mansion

Meadow pastures were my destination at twelve,
dreaming I was Trixie Belden, detective, and
Clearwater Creek's hills were upstate New York
where hidden mansions waited to be explored.

My spring pasture is full of nocturnal creatures' burrows.
Their soft mounds hide subterranean castles. Excavated clay
smothers alfalfa, big blue stem, little blue, gamma.
Topsoil obstructs sunlight's warm breath.

Rodents prefer sweet, aging alfalfa thatch
to build dens that in turn provide beds
for noxious thistle seeds and other weeds -
unholy unions ruin land for grazing and hay.

Terraced hills are wagon trains circled for the night,
winter's melt fights to break the rings, creates
ideal conditions for hefty underground dwellers
excavating homes in the terraformed mounds.

Tunnel entrances are big enough to swallow a horse's leg.
Unaware, a person can break stride, easily step inside
Alice's rabbit hole for an unplanned journey
to another world.

I head to the pasture these days to think though
thorny problems, replace rotted posts, tighten wires,
cut thistles, and imagine my life
in a secret manor house.

Flowers Don't Frolic

It was my turn to name the new foal,
fifth in a line of tall strapping colts

and fancy fillies that grew into beautiful
quarter horses,

all born to a fine-stepping mare
and an ordinary-appearing stud

with champion bloodlines.
I named the new foal Kenny

after my recently deceased father
and mourned Dad again,

when the two-month-old colt twisted his gut
in a freak accident and died.

I lost my appetite for horse breeding,
concentrated on raising vegetables

and flowers that don't frolic or run in circles
around their mothers until they fall.

Skylining

He has a tendency and a talent,
if truth be told,
to name places, situations,
and categories,
like teasing me about hiring
local electric or plumbing contractors.
He called the group of them
little men from the village.
He described locations,
like an intersection with corn
growing in every field
where frequent accidents occur,
lost sodbuster's corner,
and like a friend who rides his horse
ahead of the herd
is always described
as *skylining.*

Naming poems, stories, or a section
of the pasture,
for that matter,
is one of my biggest challenges,
almost on par with
my lack of technical skills
to replace a barn door handle,
add a yard light by the shed,
or repair a broken
underground livestock water line.
I'll call
an electrician, a plumber,
a carpenter, and other helpful
experts from the village
every time.

Fencelines

after Sue Wallis' *Timothy Draw*

We pause at the top of Timothy Draw
although these clay hills have mostly gulleys,
this ravine was named after an old codger
that lived down there a generation ago.

He liked to name geographic oddities,
tributaries no maps claimed, corners
where accidents occurred and even
paddocks in a divided pasture.

Without realizing it, or giving credit,
we use those names too, for utility.
Wedding Hill where Zeke and Molly
exchanged vows, Sodbuster's Corner,

frequent location of car accidents
between three corners of corn and this
hilly pasture, the Loadout where semis
pick up and drop off momma cows.

Zeke, of this new generation, lays claim
to fence lines, setting posts to make them
last. He uses discarded rural electric poles,
or new creosote ones, strings four stands

of barbed wire and an electric line,
protects those fences from cows leaning,
grabbing grass always greener outside,
intends them to last our lifetime.

Gates

A cussin' woman's a trial to hear
for folks who want to think
that females ought to smile the while
a skunk is making stink. – Gwen Petersen, *A Cussin' Woman*

It was plain for her to see which gates
should be open for calves to flow
from the grove where they bounded,
lost when herd moved out to pasture,
mommas making a righteous noise.

He plainly disagrees, opens a gate
she just closed, explaining he wants
to give calves plenty of room,
avoid bunching, breaking hot wires.

Both theories work, she supposes,
cussing his stubborn streak, sure
he didn't hear, his hearing such as it is.
He concedes she is probably right,
but only after moving cows his way.

He Usually Writes It Down

Wisely and slow; they stumble that run fast. – William Shakespeare,
Romeo and Juliet

We all forget names, places, and events as we age,
signs are all around if one can remember to notice.

I sometimes forget why I walk into another room,
wonder if I locked the door last night, and worry

I will neglect to turn off my coffee pot or stove,
burn down the house like old people in the news.

A rancher checked cattle and horses here the other day,
failed to close one gate and left the rest unlatched.

He usually writes everything down, keeps notes
in his pocket but forgot to check his list that day.

I make a circuit after he leaves, checking gates,
locking them again to keep livestock in.

Another friend adds events to his phone calendar,
but forgets to look at it; he made a date Thursday

morning for Friday evening, then arrived that day.
He does not recall birthdays, places visited last year,

or people he met. Lately, he forgets his wallet
and driver's license. I worry about him

having an accident, but can tell him anything;
it is like locking secrets in Fort Knox.

Mare's Dance

In the summer two mares and two geldings
graze together, nicker when they see a farrier.
They politely share winter oats and prairie hay.
Separated now to test motherhood's surprise
likelihood, the mares Jody, and Big Diz try
grazing awhile on fresh tender fescue,
then return to the rickety wood barrier
separating them from their gelding allies.

Jody sighs during the trailer-ride, alights
at a run, raises her tail, twists to the right,
sashays to the gate that splits the lady
from a potential mate on the other side.
Her winking vulva signals her intention
to get this stud's undivided attention.

Grass Glistens

Life goes by fast. Enjoy it.
Calm down. It's all funny. – Joan Rivers

Moon and stars blush pink,
hide behind storm clouds
lingering until May's morning
hides them for another day.
Grass glistens with water drops.
Roses bloom. Peonies droop.
Just-mown lawn grows an inch.
Cat jumps on my lap, track's
sand from summer's cellar fix,
leaves footprints on my t-shirt.
Horses' coats shine from their
recent bath, and the sheepdog
worries about more thunder
that hurts her tender ears.

Horses Moon

Grey and yellow barn cats perch
on dusty saddles in June
under the light of a new Horse Moon.
Mostly green eyes narrow to slits,
gaze toward the half- door
as the nearly white Appaloosa
thrusts his head into the tack room
in search of oats.

Forty-five Mommas, Forty-four Babies

The ultimate luxury in life remains nature. – Robert Rabensteiner

Cows and calves arrive early Sunday morning,
leave the semi-trailer mooing.
Mammas call their babies, *come here, come now.*
Mares and one lone gelding run along fence line,
excited for, yet divided from, new arrivals.
Fog blanket covers them next morning,
quiet after a long week talking, except for sporadic
babies' calling mamma, *I'm hungry.*
One mamma mourns loss of her calf silently,
grazes among the pairs.

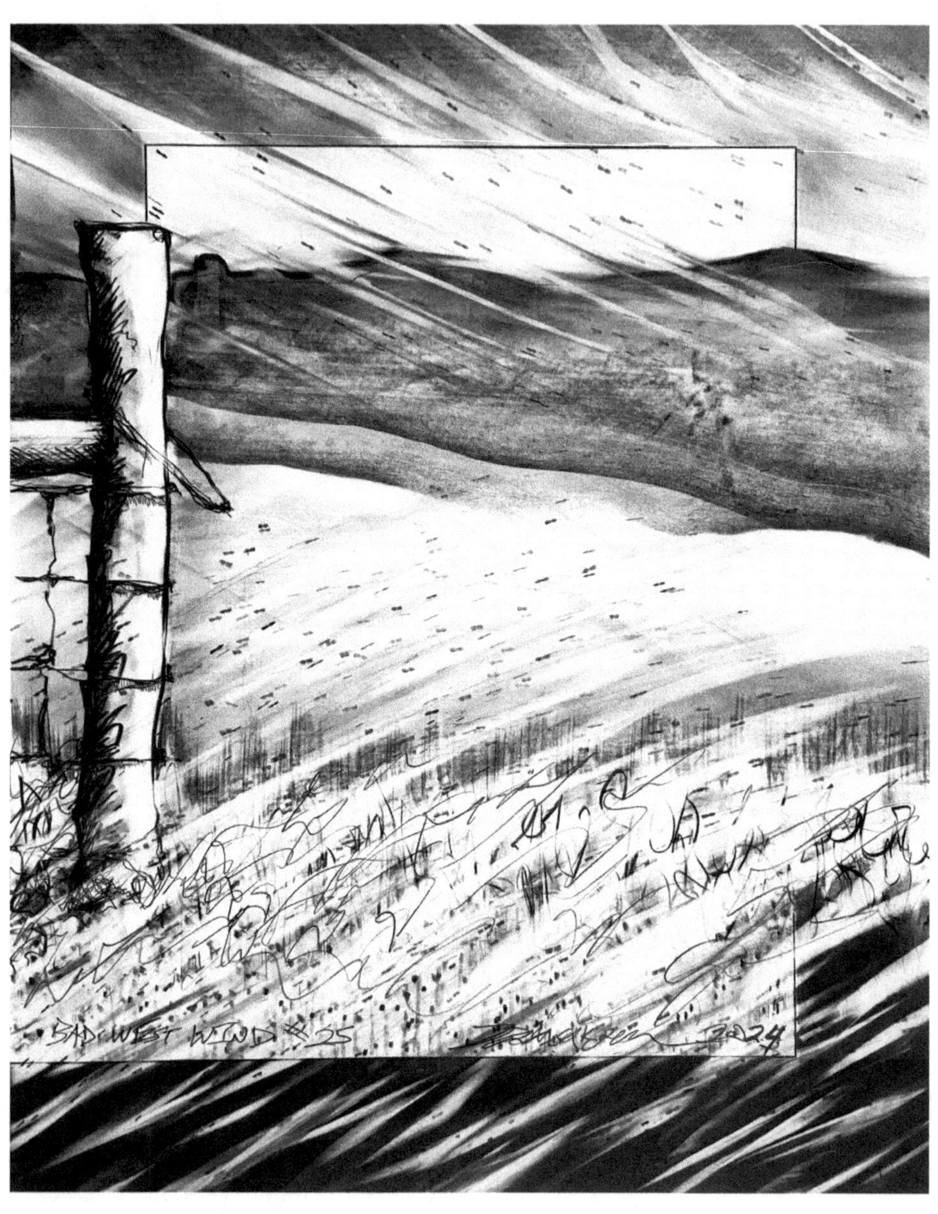
BAD WEST WIND #25
2024

Summer Foals

Imagine a fine vineyard
on these grasslands,
a vision of distant black and silvery leaves,
summer foals frolicking nearby.
Della Mae Akers, a new grape,
flourishes on the hill;
sun shines on the vines.
Red wine smiles on my tongue,
where the nose is ripe and fruity
with plumbs and dark fruits,
served with beautifully marbled cheese,
blue veins woven through the curd.
Hear the mares' nicker to their young.

A pretty dream, but how,
when walking pipes,
corn crops, finite water,
neighborhood white noise
drowns my voice and
politicians are a charging herd?

Night falls, bentwood chairs
beckon me to the table.
Trees show distinct profiles
in the moonlight, shield my view
from the neighbor's shiny silver
water sprinklers.

Mimi, pour another glass of wine,
s'il vous plait.
Let's forget for a time and dream
this plains landscape into our home.

Barn Dust Meditation

Dust covers barn spiders' webs
that hang from rafters; trapped
prairie hay wisps form designs
like a dry country Hydra.

> *Focus on the broom, sweep spider webs,*
> *clean barn walls, sort metal bolts, burs,*
> *lift with my legs to avoid back strain,*
> *breathe one breath, then another, and another.*

Filth replenishes daily from topsoil
riding jet stream winds, dislodges
from muddy horse hooves, cats' paws,
alfalfa bales, oat particles, and feed sacks.

> *Ignore dust swirling around saddles, bridles,*
> *settling on horse blankets,*
> *my father's timeworn and dried-out*
> *leather team collars and driving reins.*

I breathe moldy powder disturbed
during barn cleaning; grime sneezes
out or sifts through my lungs
and lodges in my sinuses.

> *Watch webs full of straw crumbles and see*
> *blankets covered with prairie hay bits filtered*
> *through imperfect hay loft floors. Step outside*
> *regularly for breaths of fresh air.*

My aching muscles bend to the task
of shoveling dried horse apples, aging straw,
and years-old dirt into wheelbarrows to mulch
asparagus, rhubarb, tomatoes, peppermint.

Prepare dinner of grilled veggies, rhubarb-mint pie.
Serve it on a deck overlooking flowerbeds free of dust.
Chase it with a glass or two of single malt scotch
to cleanse throats and clear sinuses.

New Alfalfa

When hay is cut,
then a heavy downpour
before it leaves the field,
it ruins alfalfa for the season
like it did one year
and Goldilocks moved on.
No money for farmer,
no food for horses
or cows come winter
and higher costs to import.

When haying season is just right,
like last year, hot and dry,
Goldilocks decided to stay.
Hay farmer made bales,
dropped them in the field
at a perfect time.
Hay accumulator machine
loaded multiple squares
on the hayrack at once.

Crew was dusty, dripping sweat,
needing multiple
hydration breaks,
Goldilocks watched from afar.
They unloaded stacked bales
safe into barn before incoming rain.
We all inhaled sweet scent
of fresh alfalfa.

I handed out iced tea,
cokes and other sodas of choice,
ice water,
ice cream cones, dilly bars,
and watermelon slices.
Necessary aid when heat index
hits ninety-plus like it was that day.
Goldilocks smiled, *it's just right.*

Goodnight, Monkey

Strawberry roan colt
rollicks around his mother,
among the legs

of his older sisters and brothers,
entertains all with his
monkey shines.

He's sixteen hands tall,
golden mane and tail
shine in morning sunlight

like polished brass.
Undisciplined (though we try),
he wants to be my friend,

but like a big kid who doesn't know
his size, shoulders others aside
for more than his share of hay,

oats, and a turn in the barn
as easily as I can toss
throw pillows to a couch.

His long-legged stride
easily propels him forward
like an outboard motor

powering a tiny rowboat.
Once saddled, he jumps sideways,
crow-hops and bucks

like he's training for a rodeo,
and always looks surprised
when the rider is thrown,

having taken no notice
of the weight on his back.
On a horse trailer tonight

to a new home, he doesn't look back
as I wave and say without regret,
Goodnight, Monkey.

Beauty of the Equinox

A late sunrise ushers in
autumn's equinox.

Last of tomatoes are picked
and preserved for winter.

Temperature is below forty
first time since last spring.

Sun's early rays warm house
and soul this lovely morn.

It's quiet here with cows gone
to winter pasture.

I catch my breath from summer's
last hectic rush to harvest.

Yet, there's always something
unpredictable.

We moved horses to the south paddock
the day before a lightning storm.

A sixteen-hand gelding named Dutch
is killed by lightning strike.

We bury him in the pasture
next to the spot he fell

in shadow of a giant wind tower,
within sight of a dozen more.

Other horses avoid his burial mound
instinctively knowing a taboo.

Even amid sorrow, I want to tell
of this equinox morning's beauty.

Can't See the Beauty

Walking through the pasture,
eyes on the ground
searching for thistle regrowth,
gallon of poison spray in hand,
I watch for nocturnal prairie-critter
burrows wide enough to catch a foot
or turn an ankle,
deep enough to fall inside,
almost miss this fine autumn day.

Finally navigate past a warren,
look up to witness late afternoon sun
filter through thin clouds,
highlight ashes' gold leaves,
horse-chestnuts' red,
locust's bright yellow,
green rustling-leafed cottonwoods
towering above.

Long-sleeved-t-shirt perfect,
sun just warm enough
to ripen a few last tomatoes.
Remnants of late summer flowers
host occasional bumble bees
clinging to gently swaying blooms.

I share this gift of a day by selecting
the last of the yellow-delicious apples
grounded in a recent breeze
with horses impatient as kids
lining up for ice cream cones
on the 4th of July,
jockeying to be first in line.

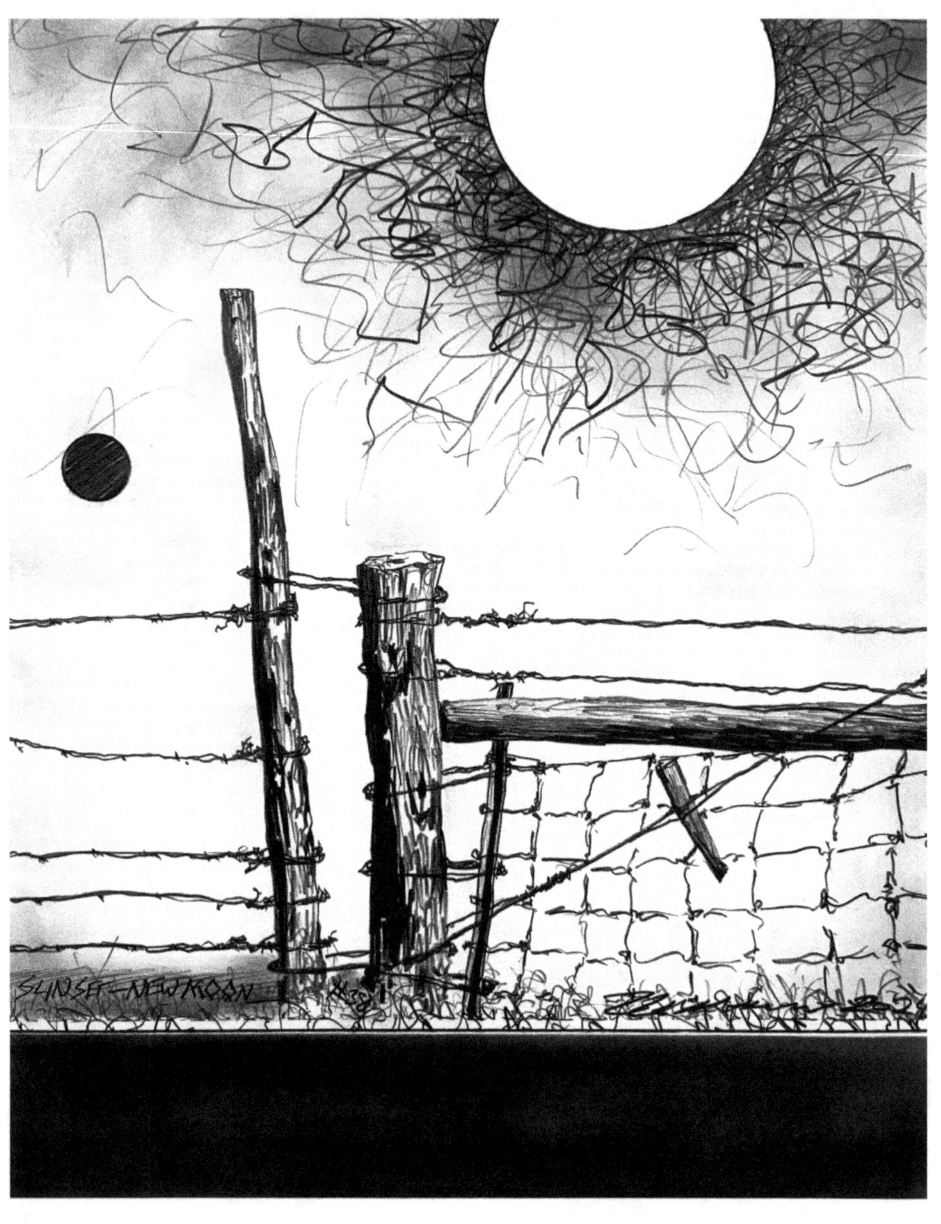
SUNSET—NEW MOON
#38

Sand Pastures in Autumn

Genetic memories of sandbur-filled
blowouts and brown buffalo grass
fill my dreams after a day
when shifting sand plugs postholes
as fast as we dig them,
slowing the hurry to finish one more
fence this fall and keep our horses
from a neighbor's mature crops.

Goldenrod and tall spreading sunflowers
invade ditches and over-grazed pastures.
I long for cultured cottage gardens
with late season lavender and pink asters,
multitudes of purple bell flowers hosting
honeybees, monarchs, swallowtails,
enough buttercups to bring smiles.

I dream of beaches during drought,
water of all kinds – lakes, rivers, ponds, oceans,
cattail and willow-covered wetlands,
wake with the taste of dust.

Cunning

Curious fox looks my way
when I open church door
across from old courthouse,
set out the counseling sign.

He stands still, watching me.
I run to grab a phone to record,
but fox is gone slap-dash.

Later the same autumn morn,
raven perches on identical bit
of lawn, watches door open-wide
to a prompt knock, rises in flight,

circles, disappears out of sight,
mystically, like fox fled earlier,
leaving me to ponder destiny.

Nebraska Dry

When I find myself in times of trouble,
Mother Mary comes to me
Speaking words of wisdom,
let it be. – Paul McCartney

I fished a dead possum from the horse tank last week.
Son finds another one this week, empties the befouled water.
The marriage of water-seeking wildlife during a drought
and clean water for horses is an unhappy union.
I pick and dry rosemary from this summer's crop.
Scent lingers on my fingers, takes me back to a taco-buffet
birthday for a friend. People come and go as people do.
Strangers across the table from him and me bow their heads,
softly pray to Mother Mary. Chatting, we find past neighbors
and hometowns in common, that we were taught by the same
rural teacher, recently deceased. The couple asks how many kids
and grandchildren we have. *We're not married* we both answer.
I'm quiet. He reveals that he got an annulment from his mother-church
to marry a second time, decides not to do it again.

I don't intend to tell my divorce story, steer conversation
back to our common interest. Rural teachers were only required
to have teaching certificates years ago, like my maternal grandmother.
She was a teacher until 1914 when forced by her local district
to quit when she married. In the 1960's when our mutual teacher
taught me, he had taken classes but not enough to graduate.
The rural teacher and I both completed bachelor's degrees in '73.
That teacher instructed the man across the table, too, but years
after teacher earned his credential. There've been dry spells since
we attended rural schools; however, no one recalls a drought this bad.
Machines spark grass fires; high winds flare them. Storm cloud funnels
form, tornados sirens blow, send us to our separate cellars.
We turn on the automatic waterer to provide horses' fresh water.
Wildlife perches on its ledge to drink.

Milky Way

Forgot to turn on the yard-light
before I left home on a bright
sunny afternoon, neglect
to think about how early dark
arrives now that time has turned.
Home late from a grocery run, I
will need to unload in the morn
when light returns, roll my eyes
as if to ask myself, *Where was*
your head? Make my way to barn
to feed cats and horses. Take in
night's starry sky, the breathtaking
Milky Way, illuminating the dark
like a sheltering canopy overhead.

Bales Topple

"From now on," he said, "I don't want anyone to come to see me while I'm here. Is that clear?" – Joseph Heller, *Catch-22*

Horses don't recall when they last ate,
rush to check new additions to the menu,
ears alert for rattling gates and water

flowing from hydrant to tank.
Like Major Major, I like to feed horses
when they are not here.

Five of them crowd me,
starved since their last meal
last night or ten minutes ago.

When they wander out to pasture
daily to check if anything green
grew since the last check eight hours

or ten minutes ago, it's feeding time.
Bunks built next to barns
ease my fear of trampling, allow

oating, haying without five curious noses,
twenty running feet, three ton of horse flesh
pushing, shoving, playfully bucking.

Bales toppled from barn
into a spacious bunk offer
plenty of room for me to pitch hay,

stack flakes near boundary planks.
Equines jockey for position,
fight to be alpha horse today,

finally settle into a line.
Graceful heads dip, grab a bite,
lift mouthful aloft, chew.

Fresh Prairie Hay

Vacillating between anxiety
and hilarity at the absurdity
of the day when one client failed
to show for an appointment and
pandemic-temporary minister
stepped into my office to lay claim
to my time without permission.
Alone at home, my solo laughter
echoes across the barn's ample loft
as I select a prairie hay bale
from the careful stacks to pull it
from an upper ledge to the hayloft floor.
I climb down from the stack, drag bale
with a long red bale hook toward
sliding door, snip wire bale ties,
toss hay slabs into feeder, watch
three mares shove the lone gelding.
Feed him separately, sit on a bale,
look out into approaching evening,
inhale fresh hay's aroma, breathe.

Purpling Bluestem

Autumn whistles in some day when I'm
riding the grey gelding
bringing in fat calves for sale:
the air quick-chills, grass turns brown. – Linda Hasselstrom, *Seasons in South Dakota*

Phlox and mini hollyhocks bend their tall heads,
worship rainwater falling like autumn leaves on late blooms.

Sour dock and buffalo burr genuflect,
give thanks for another round of rain to replenish them.

This gardener will clip spent plants hanging
over sidewalks, let the remaining flower seed-heads stand.

Fall chill will be with us much too soon,
horses munch last of the purpling bluestem and rye grass.

Technically It's Not Winter Yet

Jet Stream takes the express elevator
down, way down to Texas;
mid-November, decides to stay
another week or two.
North Wind does not care he's stranding us
twenty or thirty degrees too cold.

Frigid gale scatters snow north,
spreads cold coast to coast.
Wind turbines roar to angry life again,
northwest wind booms through blades,
interrupts my sleep.

Horses stomp, paw the frozen
corral clay waiting for alfalfa.
Sparrows and downy woodpecker
hang from perches,
empty feeders at record speed.

Housecats and sheepdog make
figure eights under my feet,
run back to wood stove heat,
wait for breakfast, pester me
to keep fires blazing.

Houseplants and I perk up when sun
peeks from behind racing clouds,
warming the Thanksgiving table.

How Old Was Blue?

She is just three.
Weaned again.
First time from her dead mother . . . – Linda Hussa, *The Blue Filly*

Norfolk Livestock Sale Barn
was a going concern in the eighties.
We were horse shopping there the day
a roan gelding named Blue was for sale
from a cowboy with a broken-down
trailer needing to earn a few bucks.
We made the deal in the parking lot,
no arguing or fussing, he agreed to terms,
horse, for me this time, to join the herd.

He delivered Blue to our place after dark.
Cowboy told us horse was ten
but we think a few years older.
He'd been worked hard in a feedlot,
needed rest to regain his breath. I
often found him stretched out asleep,
imagined him as a baby born out west.
Maybe his mother died, left him an orphan
and he was mothered by a spotted burro.
Every swish of his tail told a story
of hardship as he adjusted to an easy life,
occasional cattle drive or trail ride.

Saddling Blue

Inexperienced riders
are safe on Blue. He's learned
many tricks to evade people,
as once caught, he must cope
with the latest dude.

He dodges left, then right,
turns his head from the halter
at the last moment
when it's a sure deal this attempt
will be a successful one.

Once captured he's patient
as greenhorns brush winter dust,
remove burs or hoist
the saddle to his back,
tolerates times when a stirrup

catches under the fender,
stands still for breast strap
and stirrup length adjustments.
Changing from halter to bridle
proceeds smoothly most days.

Blue doesn't like to travel alone
or lead the pack
but can follow the herd
with sure-footed,
albeit slow, speed anywhere.

Bonding

She sighs into her oats,
her breath warms my hands
as we stand together
in front of the barn.

He always hayed the horses,
took oats to the mare,
mended the tack,
when we were a couple.
Since he's gone,

I'm learning mare care.
She is patient with my fumbling
attempts to guide her nose into a halter,
waits for me to buckle the strap.

She stands untethered,
munches quietly,
eating oats set out for her
to nurture the new life
growing silently inside

her slowly-expanding belly
now off limits to rigging,
riding, ranch work.

I brush her luxurious mane,
lean my head against her withers,
pat the dust from her chestnut coat,
readying us both for times to come.

Equine Shine

November to April
horses eat hay, oats,
occasional apples.
Come May,
even loyal grooms
want to go play.
Brome grass shoots
a foot in days.
Winter hair drops
away with each
brush stroke,
dust roll,
hour on fresh spring
pasture.
Bellies full,
their coats gleam
in spring sunshine.

Rosinate Band

I watch from the comfort of my warm house on a below zero January day,
two pickups slowly drive
down the snow-covered south hill.

Trucks carry four armed men dressed in coveralls and hoodies.
Men jump from barely-halted trucks,
dart toward the ditch to find their prey.

The first shooter's free hand shields his eyes from the icy glare,
his dominant hand cradles
a long-barreled loaded rifle.

His shots into the morning sun miss the moving target,
two more pickups top the hill
and slide to a stop behind.

More armed fellows pile from their trucks like a swat team
called to a riot and more shots are fired
into Verneal's fallow field.

Just across the road in my pasture, old horses' scatter.
The blind one and the arthritic one run away
as best as they can.

Scene unfolds like a cartoon, Wile E. Coyote darts past the hunters'
spray of bullets and escapes into my pasture
among the old horses under the No Hunting sign.

Sleepwalking Rodeo

I was wakened at two
from a winter night's nap
to bang, bump, bump,
and breaking glass.

Ten-year-old son,
also awakened by the clatter,
and I arrive
in the hall together.

His father is sprawled
head down at the bottom
of the stairway,
glass fragments

and fractured family photos
framing him, one elbow
folded around the newel post,
his saving grace.

He shakes his head to clear
glass pieces from his hair,
muttering, *I was going to the bathroom,*
must have taken the wrong turn.

It was so funny to see him like that
but I knew it was wrong
to laugh at his upside down
predicament.

Son and I help him rise, return to bed
unhurt. Grinning to myself
I sweep up debris.
It wasn't his first sleepwalking rodeo.

Each Time He Was Down

He's a stubborn man,
insisted on everything his way,
ran with a fast crowd,
always a pretty woman
on his arm
except when illness or injury
stopped him.
I took him to see a doctor
each time he was down with strep
and a high fever,
when the appaloosa threw him
so hard he couldn't breathe,
and this morning in a dream
his foot slipped from a stirrup mid-mount
and he fell in a heap under the feet
of three milling horses.

Moore Peppy Kid AKA Rosie

My spring travel to the Big Apple
is interrupted by a NYC blizzard,
plane detoured to the Detroit airport
where I found an old copy of *Plumb Lucky*
in the lady's room.
Weather-stranded,
thumbing the dog-eared novel,
I called home.

My son said Rosie was sick,
mare too old and thin to recover.
He put a bullet between her eyes,
sat with her on a hillside,
toasted her long equine life
with a bottle or two.

I'm plumb lucky
to return home safely,
visit that hillside,
enjoy graveside solitude,
say my good-bye
to Moore Peppy Kid, AKA Rosie,

see her chestnut hide
shrinking back over rib bones,
curved as the Brenna Precinct hills,
once-proud head cradled in winter grass,
momma cows grazing nearby
with watchful eyes
on their early spring babies,

I catch a scent of new blooming
wild plum.

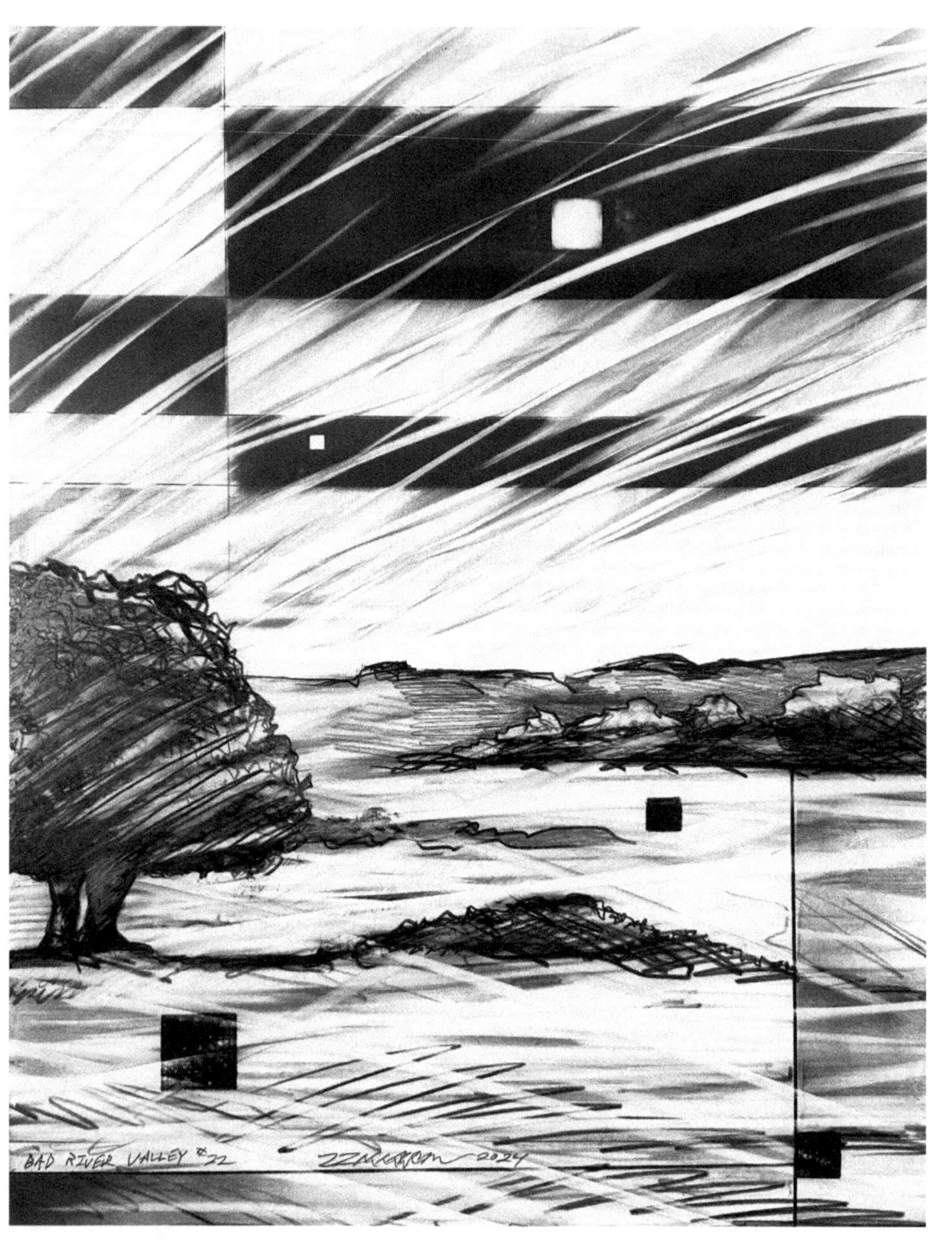
BAD RIVER VALLEY #22
2024

A Mare's Tale

Bay mare backs out of the trailer, whinnies
to the blind appaloosa and old chestnut
quarter horse aimlessly stomping flies
like drunks waiting for a bar to open.

Son and I brush against five-foot-tall
purple phlox and pale-mauve milkweed
blossoms with scent as intoxicating
as elder flowers in full bloom.

He doesn't notice flowers in a single-minded
resolve to get horses to newly-fenced pasture,
halters the blind one and I take the mare,
but she soon outpaces me, and we trade.

Mare, halter-free, explodes into a run,
quarter horse follows. Appaloosa, left behind,
whinnies for them. Horses charge across
a big-bluestem and clover meadow.

Monarchs, swallowtail, and thousands
of Sulphur's flit around us, rising
in hoof-stirred clouds, lighting this
twilight meadow like downtown Omaha.

Son runs to intercept runaways galloping
toward his new fence line; appaloosa,
far behind, calls for them, but neighbor's
diesel irrigation motor drowns sound.

Turning them in time, son halters
the gelding, leads him toward his blind
companion and walks both to a quiet corner.
Lead mare explores new pasture alone.

Deworming Horses

Leaning on my crooked walking stick,
I listen to a vet's lecture about equines'
susceptibility to parasites.

Annual deworming with a commercial
product necessary to prevent illnesses
and deformity. Alternate with a separate
paste product the next time.

Estimate the horse's weight, set
applicator syringe to match. Naming
and preparing vet supplies are easy,
getting the horse to swallow

a chalky-tasting, toothpaste-like
substance is the hard part.
First halter the horse(s). The dark
gelding is easy going, contradicting

our notion of the erratic dark horse.
The beautiful but anxious palomino
mare is jumpy. It helps to have two
sets of strong arms; one person

to firmly grasp horse's halter,
knowing the mare will jerk her head
back sharply when nasty-tasting
wormer hits taste buds.

These days it's hard to find help
for these two-person tasks. We hire
where we can. Today, it's a retired
cowboy and a weekend pirate.

While the cowboy holds the halter,
the pirate strong-arms the animal,
pry's open equine's mouth and squeezes
a syringe full of wormer

into opening behind those big teeth,
quickly feeds a bucket of horse candy – oats –
to help the equine medicine go down.

Wayne County Line Dust

Chestnut mare, oldest of Rosie's offspring,
munches oats with her younger sister
and brother, like skilled line dancers
moving in unison, in a rugged corral
on the county line. The trio bob noses
into the bunk to grab a bite, lift nearly-
matching heads, chew in harmony
like their actions are choreographed
and practiced. Her brushed coat shines
as if road dust doesn't settle on her
fine withers like it does on my Chevy
when I drive the line to visit.

Mothering-up

I walk slower...
steps more uncertain
as I follow the cow path
to the sandy creek bed. – Ruth Daniels, *Cowpaths*

I hear them from the house,
mothers calling for their young,
reminding me of my adolescent years
gathering Holsteins for milking
as I walked Clearwater Creek paths.

These Hereford momma cows call
their calves at dawn,
reminder it's breakfast.
Calves a week from weaning
bend down to nurse.

Nearly as big as their mothers,
they run and play all day
like kids on an extended recess,
escorted by a babysitter cow assigned
via innate bovine pecking order.

Unaccompanied mothers, worn down
from nursing their big babies, sleep
mid-day, take time for water breaks
or graze at ease. Serious mothering-up
occurs at dusk.

The mothers moo loud and long,
maternal reminder to adolescent calves.
Time to gather in, get close,
let us protect you a bit longer.

Patience

After Doris Bircham's, *Coffee Row*

They gather each morning –
heads over the board fence
waiting for me to finally stir.
I head to the barn, open oats
barrel, measure out a gallon
each, add a pinch of sweet feed,
trek loaded bucket to the rail,
spread grain across two
bunks to give them plenty
of room to spread out.
Even with that, the three
mares jockey for space.
The lone gelding trained
in a feedyard waits his turn.

Rain Maker Names Word Sender

"Now and then the voices would come back
when I was out alone, like someone calling me,
but what they wanted me to do I did not know." – John G Neihart,
Black Elk Speaks

Sleep evades me as low-pressure builds.
I yearn to find the right words to tell
this story, get out of bed at two am,
search for inspiration, find a drawer full

of hair ribbons, colorful as the rainbows
Black Elk saw on a mountain top after
the sky darkened and rain he called for fell.
The miracle earned him the title, Rain Maker.

John G Neihardt, in his writings, describes
talks with Black Elk around a campfire.
The chief details his dream vision as he spins
his story to Neihardt, he named Word Sender.

I quilt a version of Black Elk's vision
in comfort of my home, without hardships
John G encountered getting to Black Elk's
camp, staying for months to hear his story.

Today Thunder Gods from the west sound off,
like in Black Elk's vision, warriors ride
black horses, carry spears flashing lightning,
bring much needed rain.

Recognition Ceremony

Kill the Indian, and Save the Man. – Capt. Richard H. Pratt,
On the Education of Native Americans

My son calls to talk about cows
and horses as I'm mentally fussing
over a decision to attend a funeral.
He mentions he's helping plan
a recognition ceremony for Umo^{n}ho^{n}
Nation children taken from their families
by white authorities and sent
to boarding schools. Those institutions
did not allow Indigenous kids to speak
their language, wear their own clothes
or practice their religion. Education
officials changed their names,
cut their hair, punished them
if they practiced important rituals.

He tells me Umo^{n}ho^{n} elders
worry morning rain will interfere
with this long-planned ceremony
celebrating survivors, recognizing
those who died away from families
not allowed to bury their dead.
I reconsider my reluctance
to drive two hours to recognize
a high school classmate's life.
Native Americans did not have
this luxury when their children
were taken to be reeducated.

Night Watch

After Gretel Ehrlich's, *The Orchard*

We go into it at night,
the sheepdog and me,
Thunder Moon overhead,

expect cows to be out,
or a predator prowling
from sounds of bellowing.

Pale moonflowers glow,
outline path beside
my garden like solar lights
line cemetery roads.

I touch a button and a string
of solar lights along fence,
another in the corncrib-
turned-gazabo,

blaze a path toward cattle tank,
overflowing where cows
knocked off the float.

We see the problem,
a calf separated from
his mother by an electric

fence baby went through,
doesn't know how to come
back to her unhappy mother.

Momma's teats are leaking,
milk falling into the soil
with the water from
the overflowing tank.

White Mulberries

Purple mulberries feed swallows, robins, and jays,
but the white mulberry's sweet juicy fruits

are honeyed summer kisses,
luring wildlife, visitors, the dog, and me to stop

and eat from the tree, or find perfect
fruit scattered under its spreading branches.

Neil stops Ghost under the tree, stands on his saddle,
eats berries from the sun-kissed upper branches.

A ground hog found the eating so good last season
he moved in under nearby cedar roots,

came out of his hole at dawn to feast
on plump berries until the sun cleared the horizon.

Last evening, I saw a momma raccoon
and four babies indulging in those white berries.

Camera's snap got their attention; they turned
ten ringed eyes toward my lens,

mom scurried away into neighbor's eight-foot corn,
two young ran down the road, two up a tree,

all back minutes later, for more.

Landscape Nightmare

Air pressure changes wake me from a fitful sleep
and a self-propelled lawn mower nightmare.
Hours, days, and weeks clipping, pruning, and mowing
lost to a murderous rider's wide blade.

Firecracker-crazed neighbors blew mostly legal
munitions all week scaring the greyhound into a fatal run.
Helpless fury of loss occupies my mind,
impending storm keeps me sleepless.

We bury greyhound on a hilltop next to the old mare's
grave site by the lone ponderosa on the Fourth of July.
Thunder and lightning next pre-dawn dwarf
Chinese-imported fireballs, rockets and shooting stars.

Heavy rainfall that follows overflows gutters,
runoff floods ditches and carves tracks roadside.
Righteous downpour settles the new grave
planted with asters, lilies, and anise mint.

West Is North, Sometimes East

She had some horses she loved
She had some horses she hated
These were the same horses. – Joy Harjo, *She Had Some Horses*

My sense of direction is cattywampus
after time in a windowless hotel room.

Reorienting every morning,
vertigo returning at night.

Room spins when I turn right,
but turning away remedies my equilibrium

like the Lunar Module landed hard
in the Pacific, submerged, righted itself.

Astronauts waited rescue like I wait
return of old horses lost in shadows.

Eight horses delivered my son, Ezechiel,
in a winged chariot, wheels on fire.

Daughter Elizabeth slipped from her steed
like lightning before a storm.

Their father was lost during a blizzard
when he rode his nag on a vision quest.

My son rides Roses Jody, spiritual granddaughter
to Jody's Feathers buried under a ponderosa.

My Blue's carcass and little Kenny
left to coyotes on a grassy hill.

Apache, first horse Zeke trained,
is buried along the west fence,

Cheyenne and Dutch interred
where they fell in a creek-bottom pasture.

Dizziness gone; I turn to a trusty mount,
nuzzling me for treats.

Saving the Horse

Everywhere on earth, I am guessing,
 people are both grieving and taking away,
loving, and killing each other. – Bill Kloefkorn

Ground is frozen a couple of feet
below the surface, top layer slippery,
old horses crowd around feeder
competing for the best alfalfa flakes.

Days are warming but cold enough
to keep this horse-lover indoors
until feeding time late afternoon
when I find thirty-two-year-old Ghost

down on her side by the hay ring
with her back wedged
against the metal frame, bad leg down
preventing her righting herself.

I call her owner; he arrives, cusses
life, and begins to dig manure
away from her struggling body, hits
frozen ground as horse fights to rise

to no avail, and I watch helplessly.
Dark now, it's time to call for assistance.
My son and his dad arrive, survey scene
by yard light and propose a solution.

Pull her away from the metal ring,
flip horse to her good leg side.
They loop her front feet with one rope,
back feet with another, and on count

of three, give a mighty tug. She's over,
sits up, eats oats, gets up on four feet,
walks away from the tussle for hay.
We toast each other and horse's health.

Saving the Man

Just days after old Ghost horse fell
and we got her on her feet, the old girl
is down again in a grassy spot by the barn.

Old myself, and unable to right the horse alone,
I phone the owner about his horse falling. He
arrives promptly to attend his equine.

He curses farmers, doctors, hospitals,
and losing his last dog. *GD farmers' dump*
poison on the land, flipping doctors
didn't help my cousin when he had a stroke.

On the drive to his cousin's funeral his friend
had a gallbladder attack. He took her to hospital
in North Platte – doctors in Valentine sent
his cousin to Lincoln by ambulance.

Why not stop in Norfolk for cripes sake? Or fly?
Cousin had more strokes on the way, was mostly dead
by the time they arrived. *GD, now my friend's deadly sick*
and doctors say she needs surgery.

What's the point of going on if they kill everything you love.
GD farmers dump chemicals, makes animals sick. Happy Dog
got the cancer from running in fields covered with GD spray,
licking her feet like any dog does and it killed her.

Maybe I should have brought the gun. But GD, Ghost
wants to get up. Dagnabbit, Ghost's struggling to live.
He and I can't move her alone. A cowboy friend
arrives with another rope.

We slip front feet in one loop, back feet in other.
On count of three, PULL, flip her back to her good leg side.
She quickly gains traction, gets up on all fours,
walks away from us. We all sigh in relief.

Thunder Gods

Humidity increases
overnight. Builds toward a lightshow,
influences even ancient horse Ghost
to stop acting her thirty-five years,
forget her bad leg. She tries to roll in tall grass.

Panic grows
when I don't see Ghost next morning.
Her companion Lucky stands alone
in the nearby pasture. I find Ghost
fallen in a ponderosa grove. Chide her
for yet another tumble. Head for help.

Movement catches
my eye as I near the gate. Look back
and she's righted herself this time –
once up, she walks rapidly toward the water tank
as low pressure builds to the storm.

Thunder fissures
open the sky. Fireworks usually hidden
from mere mortals' flash around new turbines.
Gods argue over which one controls weather
and which deity allows earth to continue turning.

Winter Hair

She came home at dusk,
tired and dusty,
smelling of sweat and horses. – Luci Tapahanso, *Yes, It Was My Grandmother*

It was hot for late September; sweaty horses still wore summer hair.

They shivered when a front arrived with chill north winds and grew
legendary heavy coats. She donned her winter Carhart's and wool hat.

In spring wind, she brushes them. Red and brown horsehair flies.
Relieved to be rid of winter wear, equines roll, one after another
in spring mud, leave the last of winter's ugly sweaters behind.

On This Hill

The Appy was from a herd
of sixty wild horses
from a western Nebraska ranch
Hoss bought when he
and the horses were young and he
fancied himself as a horse trader.
It was all before Hoss decided
to go to graduate school
and fell in love with science,
became a teacher and researcher.
We had another Appaloosa, with matching
spots, took on the new horse, named
him Junior. He was always wary of people,
dangerous to walk behind,
threw my husband,
a pretty good horseman, a few times.
We talked it over with friends,
decided to send Junior to slaughter.
Neil, another darn good horseman
offered to take the outlaw,
save him from the abattoir.
He couldn't tame
the wild from Junior either,
called him Lucky-to-be-Alive Spot,
kept him as a companion for Ghost,
his dependable mare.
Time passed as it will,
My husband left, Neil lost his pasture,
Ghost turned up lame; Lucky Spot stayed cagey.
I started boarding horses,
Kept Ghost and Lucky Spot alive
with my old horses
for another fifteen years.

Ghost at thirty-five was the first to go
last spring. Independent to the last,
Lucky Spot selected his resting place
in my undulating pasture, fell, telling me,
as only a horse can, *I will die on this hill.*

Horse Burial

Late afternoon sun shines
into my eyes as it shimmers
through a row of trees planted
close together, stockade-style,
along the west side of highway 275
like the fort in *Dances with Wolves.*
We pass them on a trip to Omaha
at sixty-five-miles-per-hour
and I feel temporarily blinded
as the sun flickers between
the trunks. It's that same light
that slices through the west grove
of ash and walnut trees, the afternoon
we bury Apache. Jerry discovers
Apache's missing for morning oats,
finds him down. All I can do
day after bunion surgery
is ride in the gator to the grove
when Doc Melissa checks him,
see how thin he looks lying on his side,
notice the signs of struggle where he
tried to rise, listen with held
breath as she says his heart's too
weak to recover, nod my assent
when she asks if she should go
ahead, watch her insert a long
needle into his carotid artery,
see a thin trickle of blood,
scarlet against his white hair,
like red rose petals
on freshly fallen snow.
A last breath, and he's gone.
Phone calls to plan his burial,
then, I watch helplessly
from the Chevy tailgate bench
near the house. Backhoe
digging in my grove

like a Tyrannosaurus Rex; its head
dipped and rising, repeatedly
eating bites of yellow clay.
Young contractor, Kay,
digs a horse-sized hole
ten feet deep and eight feet wide
to hold the twenty-five-year-old
Appaloosa gelding Apache
Zeke trained as a yearling.
A glimpse of neighbor Perry
or Jerry through those same trees
as they help move dependable
cow-horse Apache from
the grassy mound where he fell
to the grave along the west fence.
It could be Kevin Costner scouting
for food; occasional voices
that reach my backyard perch
could be wolves.

My Artistic Soul

is tired this morning,
in a dry spell
like the Exceptional Drought
covering my county.
Racing to pick fragile
veggies before frost,
repotting houseplants
that summered outside,
burying the last
of the old horses.
My brain does not feel
artistic – my soul
is on vacation somewhere.
Perhaps it is in Florida
and was washed out to sea
in the rising tide,
or maybe it's in Ukraine
volunteering and got caught
up in a bombing raid.
I'm trying to phone my soul,
ask her to come home,
messages go to voice mail.

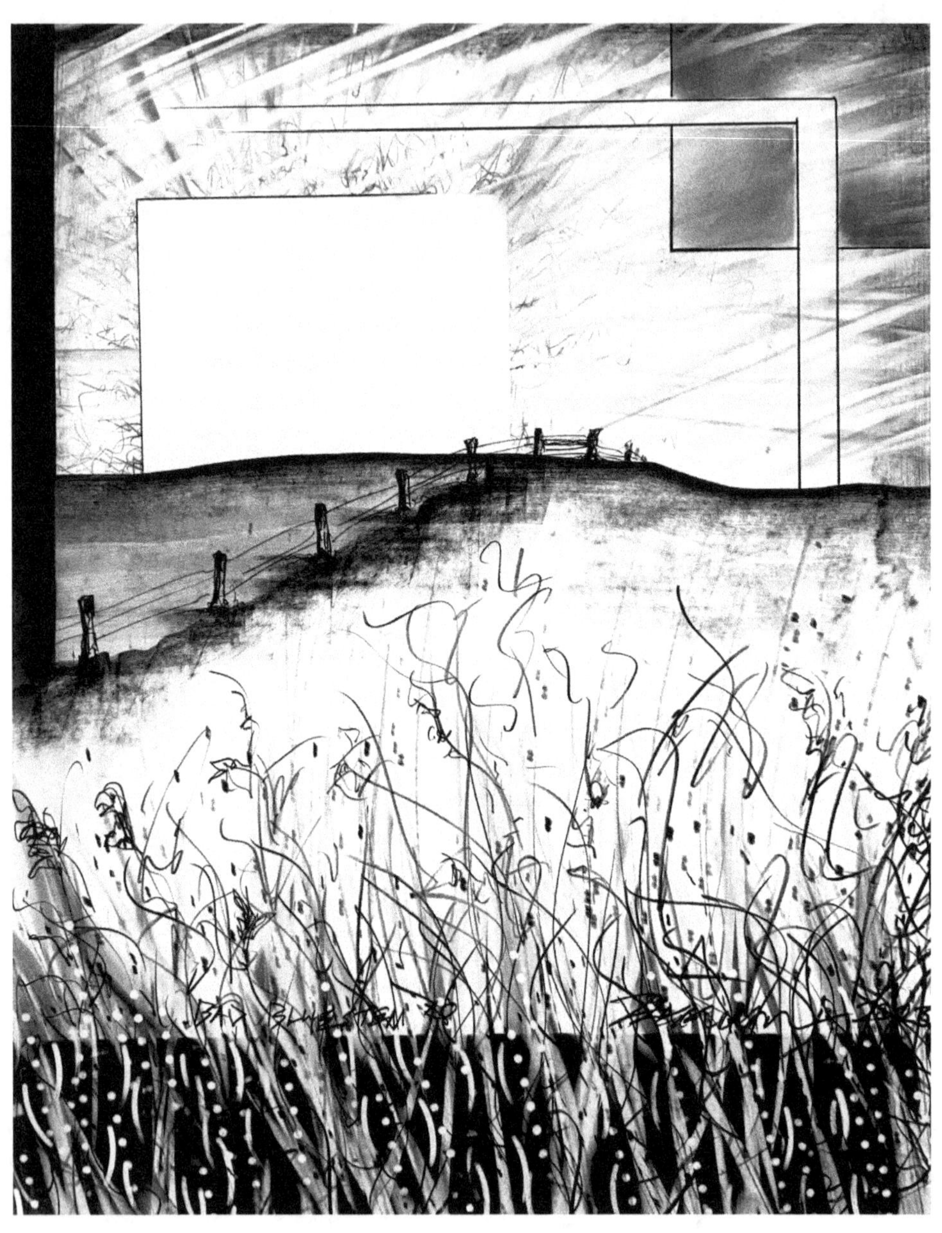

Green Barn

Barn sits at the bottom of the place
like a saucer under a cup of coffee.
Hills, cottonwood grove, horse barn,

hay shed, and saddle barns on elevations
north and west, block frigid squalls
pounding the barn. The open south door

catches pale winter sun like lepidopterists
traps moths with a butterfly net. Feed bunk
six foot lower yet, is a quiet place to pitch

hay to the horses. I take a moment, stoke
their necks and noses, listen to them
snort as they sort hay, toss flakes away,

like food critics reviewing a new café.
They look for alfalfa tidbits under prairie hay.

Write the Rain

There's something
righteous about rain
after long dry spells.

Downpours have sweet
smells and sounds
as heavy drops drum roofs,
overfill gutters.

Celebrate the rain,
even when it runs off
frozen February land
into ice-clogged rivers.

Laud the rainstorm.
Applaud the moisture.
Extol virtues of water
falling on farmland
grassland and garden.

Honor weather gauges,
gadgets and satellites.
Recognize meteorologists,
reporters and forecasters.

Pamper dogs and cats,
allow their muddy paws.
Feed horses' extra hay,
oats and barley molasses.
Keep bird feeders full.

Measure it carefully,
record it on calendar,
notebook and journal.
When wet becomes ice,
wisely balance upright
with a walking stick.

Spirits

Nothing is inherently
and invincibly young expect spirit. – George Santayana

Spirit airlines flies South
on the cheap, little room
to stretch legs, no in-flight
food or drink but it gets you
from the relative safety
of blizzards and tornadoes
to street protests in Lima,
activist clashes with military
in rural Peru, and the unknown
a mother fears. You and your
long-legged young friend fold
yourselves into those short seats,
escape North American cold,
jobs, chores, and, yes, safety
to find adventure like politicians
running from scandal. Travel
lights up your eyes, lifts spirits,
excitement you used to have
inhaling Gib's chocolate mousse,
opening gifts and playing ball.
I was bitten by the same
travel bug at about your age,
finally went on my first overseas
adventure ten years older
than you are now, to Lisbon,
my spiritual awakening.

Water Works

March corral dries
after months of snow.
Just enough daily melt
to ice at night.

One warm Saturday afternoon,
water bubbles up in horse
tracks. It's clear a pipe burst
somewhere underground.

I frantically dig trenches
to drain dung. Call, leave
message for the plumber.
Son closes the water valve.

Monday morning, plumber
arrives alone with backhoe
on a trailer, grumbles that no one
is willing to learn his trade.

He tells me he'll retire soon,
thinks he'll have to close
his business, muses about
youth who won't get dirty.

Equines watch as he drives
through their manurey corral.
The first dig through frost-
hardened clay yields *nada*.

We open valve, water percolates
to the surface to mark the leak.
He moves his rig and digs there,
stops about nine feet down.

I'm his spotter; report leakage
is spraying water, enough
to quickly fill the hole.
Digging takes an hour.

Water off again, plumber
cuts out bad pipe, clamps
a new one in minutes.
Water works again.

Old Dog, New Tricks

Thirty years is a long time
to be together – Jane Candia Coleman, *Old Pete*

First light the old mule,
that's what I call him
when I am irritated,
rises slowly from sitting,
complains of aching
bones, torn muscles
protesting his every move.

Weather forecast calls
for rain tonight, so
this morning it's time
to move near-term cows
to a different pasture,
calves due, and God
knows a storm front
will bring babies early.

Too stubborn to turn
it over to our son, his
plan is to build or buy
mounting steps to help
him heft a right leg over
the tree – once up, horse,
saddle, and he are one.

Bearing Fruit

You're impatient for the horse
barn to be finished, to begin
training your filly, yet so busy now
with teaching, cattle chores,

there's little time. Barn's not
done yet, construction like tilling
a garden in a former hog yard,
is full of unexpected obstacles.

Weed seeds germinate, rusty nails
surface, water doesn't drain.
I exchange vegetable garden spots
often for sites with more sun,

better drainage. The construction
crew goes to town for more supplies
when the materials at hand don't work,
unlike in mental health or teaching

one must work with the students
as they are. My drive to grow more
of everything made sense when you
and your sister were little but less now.

I keep gardening because veggies
don't need fences like cattle or require
showing up for midnight crises.
Gardens grow veggies in a season

in ways counseling, tutoring
new students every semester,
or training young horses
may not bear fruit for years.

Road Dust

...through swirling dust
at the back of the corral, she helps . . . – Doris Bircham, *Weaning Time*

Pulverized clay-filled air billows,
folds over in a rolling cloud
taller than ponderosa pines,
stirred by each giant machine that passes.

Dust rolls off the road, over the house,
turns black shingles dirty grey,
coats the red pasture grass,
lowers palatability, nutrition.

Farmers drive their combines
in caravans from one field
to the next, harvest far-flung crops.
Combine first, truck follows, pulls

combine's cutting head. Third in line,
a tractor, pulls the grain wagon,
so over-sized it straddles entire
gravel road, fourth vehicle brings

up the rear like a pilot car.
This day the convoy
tops the hill on the south road
across from the red grassland.

Vehicles slow and finally stop,
stacked like stair steps,
down the road. They are
forced to wait for the trailer

unloading calves after
their pre-weaning vaccinations.
Pickup and trailer
fill the road for a minute,

enough time, to slow
the industrial farm enterprise
to a five-mile-per-hour crawl,
and, for once, stop road dust.

Wet, the Good, the Bad, and the Ugly

Power surge early morning
knocks out the computer.
I set a glass of water in cup holder,
begin repair following instructions
to reboot the system,
and knock over the water.

Desk, computer mouse, key-
board, floor, and wires get soaked.
Molly stalls her mare
hoping to keep new bandage
on the almost-healed leg dry.

I use hairdryer to dry damp
useless computer mouse -
saw a real one where it shouldn't be
in the garage after returning
from Walmart with a wireless version.

Thunder this morning at five,
a brief shower morphs into rain.
Everyone has high hopes it will alleviate
a bit of this exceptional drought.

Set cup of coffee in the cup holder,
hold my breath it doesn't spill.
Young mare looks out of dry
stall, wants to roll in the mud.

A Harvest

In a dream, days pass for me without
caffeine. I am in an unfamiliar dwelling.
House dreams tell us to look inside
ourselves, do personal inventories
of our issues, problems, and concerns.
Waking, forecasters issue freeze warnings.
Twenty-seven-year-old spotted horse dies,
following deaths of Joe, Ghost, Dutch,
and Apache in the past three years.
A cold north wind signals end of summer.
Houseplants collected before frost
are full of dry leaves and mud spatters.
I pick five gallons of green tomatoes,
harvest rosemary and lavender,
fret about being a poor caretaker
for the horses in my care. A young
filly, a fifth equine, loses life's dance.
During my watch, guys with backhoes
bury five horses, four in the past
eighteen months. I wish these deaths
were all a dream like a lost coffee maker.
Rising early, I urgently want a cup
of java, mad dash downstairs.
Ah relief, coffee maker is right there
on the countertop waiting for me,
unlike the horses, gone too soon.
I feed oats to the remaining steeds.
Finally understand, no amount
of caretaking can save old horses.

It's Easier Now

Acceptance is a part of age. – Laurie Wagner Buyer, *Purple Tulips*

After a weekend of Shakespeare
offered on the green amphitheater
behind the city university, and
antique shopping with a friend

it's time to make the drive
home alone. It was unbearably
hard the first trip abroad, to Italy
that year, to return to the house,

empty except for the cats.
It's easier now and I relish the quiet.
Son brings my sheepdog home
after the weekend spent with him,

his wife, and their new greyhound.
He chored horses while I was away,
worked his pretty mare. Over coffee
he tells me that he and Junior

rode the horses around the section
on Wednesday, a four-mile excursion,
visited neighbors, pleased palomino
mare made the trip without incident.

Bright Days

Outside the bedroom window, the morning was bright and still,
save for the cool breezes and calling of birds . . . – Luci Tapahonso, *This Morning*

So much can change in a day.
I enjoy breakfast with only son
on a lovely morn, eighty degrees
before chilly rain. He brushes
his palomino's golden hair,
her coat shines like spring.
She steps sprightly, dressed
in smart wool blankets,
cushions that set off
her bronze saddle leather.
Son leads her a while
in bright sunlight before
mounting for a morning
ride around the section.

Ice Moon Jumble

Out back of Lillie's barn,
the sparse snow chills our ankles. – Jo-Ann Thompson, *Graining the Mare*

February's Ice Moon ushers
in another foggy morning,
forth in a row with freezing haze,
giving highways an icy glaze.
During morning feeding,
son's palomino mare, Freddie,
steps into a round hayfeeder.
With front feet in to snag alfalfa,
back feet out, she is stuck.
Freddie's antsy to join
other horses munching oats,
but she cannot lift her rear feet in
or back her front feet out.
Today's stunt is jumbled
in my brain with the mare's
prior escapades. One evening
last summer, she jammed
her back foot through a metal bunk
and ripped flesh to the bone.
With months of daily cleaning,
wound healed nicely.
No blood this time.
We wait for help to arrive.
My feet are cold, wish I had
a second pair of socks.
Son is sixty car miles away.
His father arrives to help,
tense from driving
slick fog-drizzled roads.
We discuss how to move Freddie,
decide to open the ring.
He asks without expectation,
Do you have any tools?
No, I answer, *just a hammer*.
He trudges to his car on slippery
snow, grabs his tool kit,

begins to remove nuts and bolts.
I stack them in neat piles,
ready to use again. Hay ring
lifts away, clearing space for Freddie
to escape. Worried from afar,
anxious to hear how she fares,
son calls. She is fine, steps out
into hazy sunshine. Day warming,
Freddie moves freely
from oats to hay, has a slushy roll,
canters to pasture and back.
We reconstruct hay feeder,
retreat to the warm house for coffee,
congratulate ourselves we did well.
However, beloved Freddie cannot
help herself. Two days later,
she sees a stray bite of hay
and steps her front legs
into the feeder. Stuck again,
imprisoned, she waits.
We repeat the job,
remove entire feeder this time.
Come spring, son moves mare
to fresh pasture to graze
on lush green. Freddie grazes
easy half the summer, leading us
to believe she is learning.
We celebrate too soon,
a storm spooks her one night
and she tangles in a fence.
Legs catch wire,
cutting deep. Vet said,
"No recovery this time,
gives the injection." Son
buries Freddie's in her pasture.

After Grief Comes Love

In the air
which moves the grass
moves the fur of a black horse
his words come back,
old griefs carried on the wind. – Linda Hogan, *Left Hand Canyon*

Breeze has calmed, wind turbines clunk,
this year, two house cats passed, sixteen and seventeen.

My sister-in-law who was like my sister
went to eternal rest during a soulless funeral service.

In equine panic, palomino startles,
runs from thunderclaps, tangles in old barbwire fence.

My son and his wife must put down
their prize golden filly after she ruins both back legs.

Grief is eating all the flowers
in our gardens and is chewing holes in the pumpkins.

It is going after neighbors' yards
and horse pastures in unchecked ugly growth.

Our grief is personal, but we have hope.
Countless people grieve after losing loved ones in war zones.

Peace does not happen automatically.
To survive grief, it will mean offering our love to others.

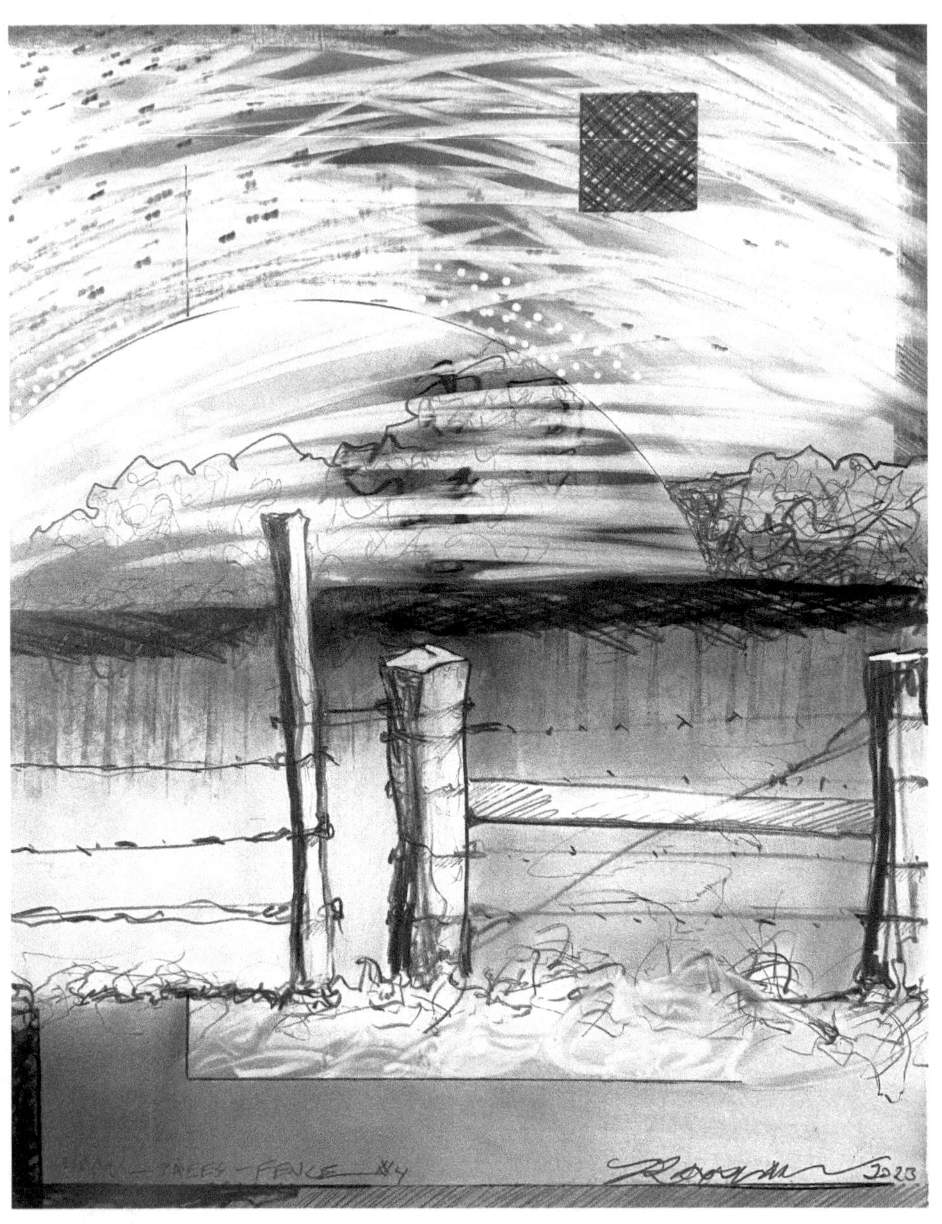
TREES – FENCE #4
2023

Horse Shopping

I often wish I could be
like my friend Carolyn, for she
is strong and she can do
most anything that she needs to- . . . – Afton Bloxham, *What Counts Most*

I've cried at every horse burial
in a backhoe-created grave
these past three years, burying

six horses, four from old age,
one sixteen-hand gelding killed
by lightning strike, and this last
death of a four-year-old mare.

It is hard to contemplate replacing
the fancy young palomino mare,
lost to us when she ruined
her legs on barbed wire.

Cows still need moving and sorting
and his old mare, Jody,
has arthritis in one leg.

She can only work in short spurts
and is best on warm days.
The palomino was supposed
to replace the older one.

Horses for sale are advertised
on websites. Shoppers can
see online parameters by location,
price, breed, or color.

They list for sale with comments,
"will ship anywhere in the US."

Peace

Wouldn't it be nice if we could all
be a little more gentle with each other. – Judy Garland

A white dove arrived
in my yard this week
to hang out with her
dove relatives.

She's here to advocate
for peace in this world
and to foster new
beginnings.

Son-in-law's father died
much too young. Family
is gathering on a Monday
to lay his ashes to rest.

The dove is a reminder
to us to be kind to each
other as we may be called
to begin again.

Bones and Ashes

We can know only that we know nothing.
And that is the highest degree of human wisdom. – Leo Tolstoy

Peer into an old pasture well
in a hundred years and you will
find bones of countless lost
raccoons, opossums, squirrels,
and rabbits that tumbled and fell.

The great owls catch bunnies,
field mice, and voles for their meals.
Their bony remains line owls' nests.

Dig into any spot on this ranch –
our dogs: Cookie, Max I, Max II,
and Sparky, are all buried here
near Wiggs' scattered ashes.
John Dog's bones rest on a hill.

Multiple barn cats and kittens
that failed to thrive, house cats –
Midnight and the special one,
Moses – are all buried in the yard.

Horses: Jody, Dutch, Ghost, Lucky,
Apache, and Blue, my fav, reside
here too. Their bones will endure
long after we all turn to ashes.

Cowhands

Where is my John Wayne?
Where is my prairie song?
Where is my happy ending?
Where have all the cowboys gone? – Paula Cole

If we're lucky, we meet two
or three savvy cowpunchers.
I've met more. Some leave life
without our permission,
others just move on.

Larry, who rode his buckskin ahead
of the herd, outlined against
the horizon, died in a car crash
with his lab puppy.

Jeffrey gave up horses
for a pretty girl, got hitched,
kids and a paying job
calving another's cows.

Buckeroo Jeff moved west
with his lady, tried his hand
at ranching until it all went
south when their baby died.

Shelia gentled big Dutch,
braided his mane and tale,
slept in her van until she met
a good man, started a family.

John was last to leave us,
a young thirty-nine, thrown
by an outlaw cayuse, trusting
he'd find good in every equine
if he just kept trying.

Memories fall over me
like autumn leaves over
pasture and corral, lucky
to have known them all.

Where Have All the Horses Gone?

You can cut all the flowers,
but you can't keep spring from coming. – Pablo Neruda

I cry over horses'
deaths, take flowers
to paint their graves.

Kenny, the sweet foal
named after my dad
died at three months

from a twisted gut –
carcass left for coyotes.
My blue roan gave

it up one fall after
untold faithful years.
His resting place

a big bluestem-covered
terrace. Apache,
the Appaloosa gelding

Zeke raised, blinded
foraging in spiky weeds
during a drought, fell,

heart weakened
after two years grazing
blind. Unable to rise,

vet put him down.
He's buried at bunkhouse
corner. Dutch, sixteen-

hand gelding killed
by a single lightning strike,
buried where he fell.

Ghost, thirty-five-year-
old Appy lay down
for the last time in spring.

She's buried in a brome pasture.
Joe, a rangy red roan fell
in a water hole in summer.

Zeke and Nick pulled him
out, but it was too much.
He's buried under swamp

oak trees nearby. Lucky,
last of the old horses,
passed peacefully under

an October sky. He's buried
in ruby-tinted little bluestem.
Death and its decay feeds

grass on horses' graves
as I hope it will feed buffalo
grass above my final rest.

Bloodlines

"Me and Franky laughin' and drinkin'
Nothin' feels better than blood on blood . . ." – Bruce Springsteen, *Highway Patrolman*

Third filly born here twenty-five
years ago, to More Peppy Kid,
AKA Rosie, and Johnny One Time,
from Hancock bloodlines.
She spun and cavorted till we
were dizzy watching her.

Name stuck, shortened to Diz.
Boarding here with Jody's Feathers,
her smaller yet two-years-older sister,
inseparable always. Jody
ran the herd, Diz her enforcer.
Horses were milling about
in pasture midday. I guessed
incorrectly, it was the gusty wind
that upset them and usually-calm
Jack, the lone gelding.

I was puttering about the kitchen,
favoring a bum leg. Diz's owner
stopped for coffee, offered help,
"Yes, please walk puppy Penny,
and check the horses."
I hobbled to the barn to feed cats,
saw him returning from pasture talking
to Zeke, who grew up with horses,
rode Diz to sort cows since
his main horse, Jody, got arthritis
in her back leg and shouldn't work.

“Diz’s dead and I called Todd
to bring his backhoe,”
he said, in the calm voice
one has before grief sets in.
Mid-October sun sets over her
prone body lying in autumn-
reddened big bluestem, above
ground one last night in pasture
where she was born and raised.
Burial first thing in the morning.

Hidden Sun

when I die
bury me on a south slope . . . – Thelma Poirer, *grasslander*

State legislatures pass rules
about dying and burying,
just like there are rules
for marrying or divorcing.
Consider, for a moment,
ignoring those conventions,
of lying down on a south slope
in the grasslands surrounding
your house, making it home
everlasting, a grave unadorned.
Buried there under,
but hidden from,
the ever-rising sun,
a place to let go of old stories,
create new ones.
You become prairie grass,
feel horse hoofs thunder above,
relax old bones under gentle massages
of bovines moving, grazing.

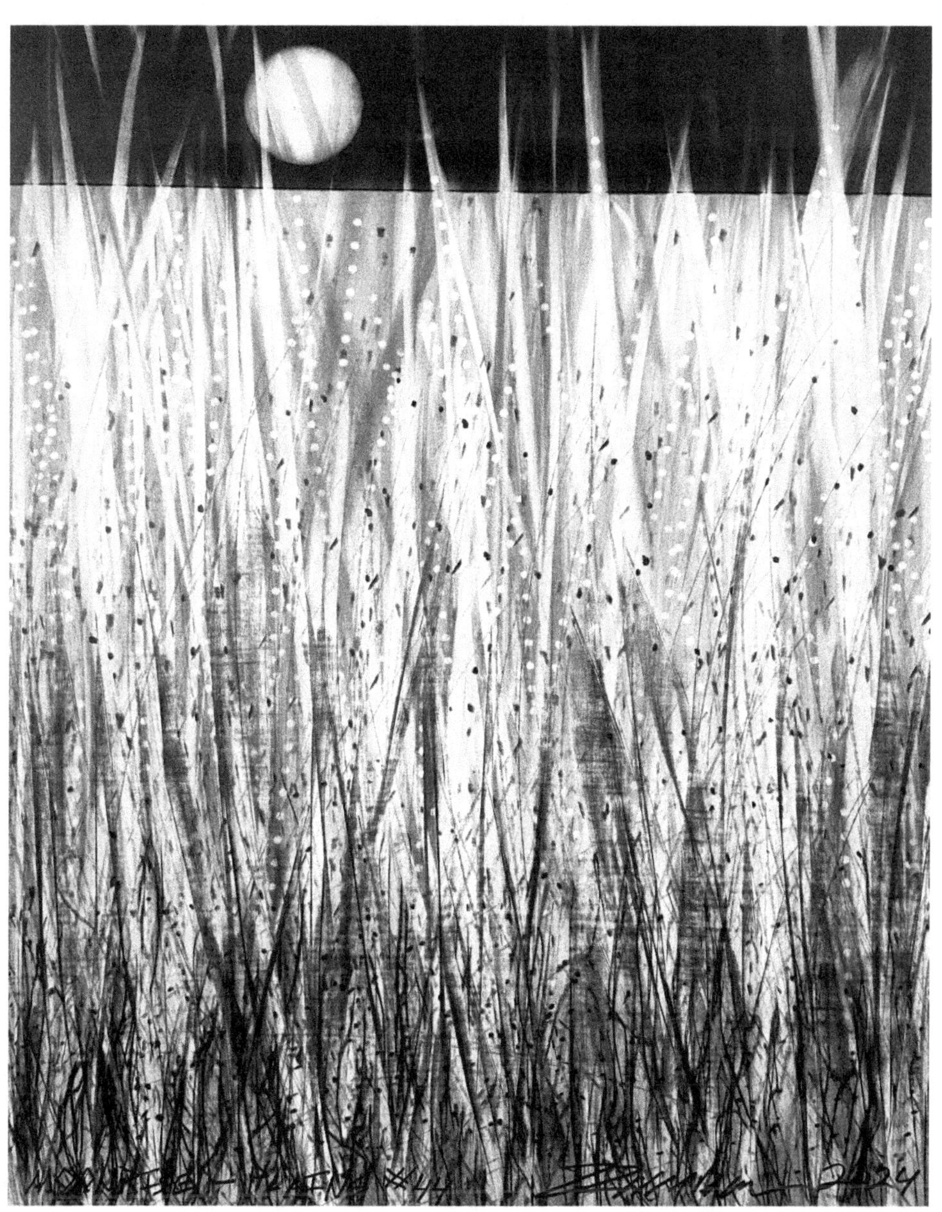

About the Author

Lin Marshall Brummels' writing and mental health philosophies are closely aligned. She believes participation in creative endeavors and spending time in nature are important for emotional wellness. She encourages her clients to seek creative outlets through an art form and/or time outdoors. Following her own advice, she started writing in mid-life after major changes. Her poems in this manuscript focus on how horses intersect with life's milestones. Brummels earned a BA in Psychology, MS in Rehabilitation Counseling, and is a licensed mental health counselor.

About the Artist

Mark Zimmerman searches the open spaces of the high plains for inspiration, journeys into the mountains for thin air, and the badlands for solace, producing abstract paintings and drawings that seek to capture the essence of Western landscapes. He searches the landscapes of the heart to write prose and poems. Mark earned a BFA and a master's degree in printmaking, as well as an MFA in painting and drawing.

Acknowledgments

I offer my sincere thanks and appreciation to the publishers of my books, and editors of journals and magazines who published poems and earlier versions of those poems. Each publication has a place in my heart.

Fine Lines Journal
"My Artistic Soul," 2022
"Rainmaker Names Word Sender," 2024
"A Harvest," 2025

Hard Times, Finishing Line Press, chapbook 2019
"Bonding"
"The Crossing"
"Horse Thief"
"Once in a Blue Nebraska Moon"
"Prairie Post"
"Summer Foals"
"Sentinel"
"Solstice Celebration"

Good Life Review
"On This Hill" 2025 TGLR: On This Hill by Lin Marshall Brummels

Nebraska Life Magazine 2019
"Rosinate Band"

Nebraska Poetry Society 2024 Open Winners | NE Poetry Society
"Gazing West," & "After Grief Comes Love," Honorable mention poems in 2024 Poetry Contest

Words in the Wind, Nebraska Writers Guild Voices from the Plains anthology, 2023
"Where Have All the Horses Gone?"

San Pedro River Review 2016
"Each Time He was Down"

Scapegoat Review 2022
"Beauty of the Equinox"

Scurfpea Publishing Anthologies
"Laced With Whiskey," 2018
"Flowers Don't Frolic," 2019
"Patience," 2024

A Quilted Landscape, Scurfpea Publishing 2021
"A Mare's Tale"
"Bales Topple"
"Each Time He was Down" & San Pedro River Review 2016
"Flowers Don't Frolic" & Scurfpea Publishing 2019 Anthology:
"Goodnight, Monkey"
"Horse Burial"
"Horse Circus"
"Horses Paint a Pretty Picture"
"Goodnight, Monkey"
"Laced with Whiskey" & Scurfpea Publishing 2018 Anthology
"Moore Peppy Kid"
"Rosinate Band" & Nebraska Life Magazine2019
"Saddling Blue"
"Wayne County Line Dust"
"West is North"

Feed the Holy online zine 2024 Three Poems by Lin Marshall Brummels
"Cunning"
"Pocket Song"
"Rhyming on Horseback"

The Prairie Review 2026
"Boodlines"

I fell in love with Teresa Jorden's anthology, *Graining the Mare, Poetry of Ranch Women.* Twenty-two of the new poems in this manuscript were inspired by the book, *Graining the Mare, Poetry of Ranch Women,* edited by Teresa Jorden, copyright 1994. The poems in this collection are timeless looks at ranch life by the women who lived the life.

Fifteen of the poems in this collection were published in my book, *A Quilted Landscape*, published by Scurfpea Publishing. An additional eight more poems were published in my chapbook, *Hard Times*, published by Finishing Line Press. The remaining poems are inspired by the horses I've known and loved.

www.ingramcontent.com/pod-product-compliance
Lightning Source LLC
LaVergne TN
LVHW010925110826
845149LV00013B/2487

* 9 7 9 8 9 9 2 8 8 4 8 3 8 *